The New Public Security Model for Mexico

The New Public Security Model for Mexico
Genaro García Luna

Primera edición, noviembre 2011

D.R. © Genaro García Luna

Derechos reservados conforme a la ley
ISBN 978-607-00-5037-4

Impreso en México
Printed in Mexico

The New Public Security Model for Mexico

Genaro García Luna

Table of Contents

For all Mexicans
Whose highest honour is to serve their country

For all those who
lost their life for the Nation.

For all those who,
through personal sacrifice and that of their families,
still work for Mexico.

Prologue[1]

Antonio L. Mazzitelli
Regional Representative of the United Nations Office of Drugs and Crime for
Mexico, Central America, and the Caribbean

In 1642 English philosopher Thomas Hobbes published the book *De Cive*, in which he developed a theory of civil society and the State to justify the transfer of certain 'natural' individual rights to the State and its institutions, including the right to justice and the defense of life and property as a means of protection from attacks by other citizens and foreign enemies. On the basis of this well-known contractual concept of the power of the State, Hobbes cited the famous Latin phrase *"homo homini lupus"* (man is a wolf to man) to highlight the need to join forces in defense against the constant threat the human condition poses to the full enjoyment of individual rights.

The debate concerning the State and its prerogatives, in particular the defense and protection of citizens' rights, has been enriched since Hobbes by the contributions of thinkers such as Locke, Spinoza and Montesquieu, and in particular the reflections of French-Swiss philosopher Jean Jacques Rousseau who published *The Social Contract in 1762*. If for Hobbes the contract between citizens was rooted in fear and the need for protection from others[2], for Rousseau it was a manifestation of the will of each individual to build a society based on justice and regulated by laws. In this respect the State and its institutions are nothing more than instruments for executing the will of the majority, expressed in turn through democratically agreed laws.

---

1. The opinions expressed in the Prologue are those of the author and do not necessarily reflect those of the United Nations.

2. *Stauendum igitur est, originem magnorum et diuturnarum societatum non a mutua hominum benevolentia, sed a mutuo metu extitisse* (One should then say that the most important and longest lasting origin of society is not found in the mutual ties of the companionship of men, but rather in the fear of others).

A contract between citizens therefore becomes *social* precisely because it is agreed upon between *partners*, that is, peers who enjoy identical prerogatives.

The societies described by Hobbes and Rousseau are certainly not comparable to today's societies, even when the concepts of "citizen's contract" and "social contract" remain popular. Whether we like it or not, today we are all citizens of the same *global village*, sharing problems with individuals living thousands of kilometers away and being exposed to risks and threats beyond our control —and over which we have little or no influence. In addition, we embrace the opportunities and the advantages offered by this *global village* to produce and trade goods and services, to travel, communicate and develop our personal skills and in this way contribute to social progress. We increasingly live, as noted by Austrian-British philosopher Karl Popper, in "open societies" where the original idea of the social contract suggested by Rousseau is inadequate to describe the multiplicity and complexity of the social, economic and political relationships that determine our lives today.

The movement of our societies towards these "open" models described by Popper, which are characterized by democratic systems of government and better opportunities for all, has also led, together with the phenomenon of economic and cultural globalization, to the development of a materialistic culture that assigns more value to money than to the moral and ethical principles of citizens. This trend emerges as one of the conditions making the growth and development of organized crime possible, with such crime becoming an inevitable component of the social fabric, altering, or rather exerting, a significant influence over the dynamics of relationships between individuals and between individuals and the State. As a result, the generalized acceptance, whether explicit or tacit, of illegality as one of the motors of society is based precisely on such a materialistic concept of existence and this frequently degenerates into the use of violence as an instrument of individual affirmation. In other words, and returning to Hobbes, *"homo homini lupus."*

Faced with this new reality, what is the role of government institutions and, in particular, the police? It no longer seems to be merely that of enforcing the law once crimes have been committed or simply protecting and guarding individual and collective interests; at least not in the more reactive sense assigned to it up until several decades ago. Societies increasingly demand that police focus on proactive schemes designed more for crime prevention than the repression and punishment of criminals. Law enforcement is increasingly required to identify, combat and destroy the complex criminal networks that characterize modern crime and which operate as veritable crime "companies." More and more they are asked to play the role of protector and aid the victims of these crimes, and they are increasingly called upon to act more vigorously as the right arm of a justice administration that is not only effective but also respects human rights and guarantees due process.

To respond to these demands, police in modern States should have adequate human resources: highly qualified and trained men and women with access to investigation and information tools in keeping with the technological developments of the modern era. Furthermore, the legal and regulatory framework should allow them to operate efficiently in a context governed by the Rule of Law, not only as a guarantee to citizens but also to provide them with clear guidelines for their often difficult tasks.

A modern police force should be formed by true security professionals, men and women with a calling who are willing to risk their lives in defense of their peers and democratic values; men and women who are, at the same time, motivated by the recognition of the society they serve and by career prospects that guarantee dignified living conditions for both them and their families. In light of the power achieved by organized crime, a trained and professional body with well-paid and socially respected officers is today a *conditio sine qua non* for the effective performance of police duties.

But a police force that embodies such characteristics is of little use if it is not accompanied by a swift and equally effective system of administering justice. In order for citizens to feel truly safe it is also essential for the State to make the principle of certain punishment a palpable reality, ensuring that criminals serve their sentences in prisons where due compliance with the purposes of the punishment are guaranteed by unrestricted respect for human rights which include, of course, the right to life and the physical integrity of those sentenced. Only in this way can the State and its institutions earn the trust and esteem of citizens which will in turn allow them to build a public and collective security together, that is, it will be the result of the joint efforts of institutions and citizens.

This book by Genaro García Luna, for which I have the honor of writing the Prologue, describes a significant number of the efforts initiated by Mexico's Federal Government, headed by President Felipe Calderón Hinojosa, to fulfill its obligation to provide security and justice for everyone living on Mexican soil. The anticipated results of these efforts represent a substantial contribution to the role that Mexico, the thirteenth largest economic power in the world, is undoubtedly expected to play in a regional and global context characterized by the expansion of illegal markets and transnational organized crime. Faced with crime that does not respect nationalities or borders, institutional responses are needed to prevent and combat criminal acts in a context of reciprocal respect, collaboration and the coordination of efforts without surrendering, of course, any of the prerogatives guaranteed by the principle of State sovereignty.

For Mexico, reform of the federal police system and the creation of a New Public Security Model in line with the present-day characteristics of criminal phenomena represent a step in the right direction. This is a step that complements reforms to the criminal justice system and it is hoped will also be supported by the corresponding reorganization and professional development of state and municipal police bodies.

Jean Monnet, one of the founders of the European Union, when referring to the process of unification of Europe and of the many obstacles that opposed such unification once said that "nothing is possible without men; nothing is lasting without institutions." Therefore, The New Public Security Model is, without a doubt, an investment in the future.

Presentation

Dr. José Enrique Villa Rivera
Director of the National Council of Science and Technology (Conacyt)
and former Director of the National Polytechnic Institute (IPN)

One of the responsibilities of any nation State is to guarantee the security of the persons and property within its territory. The text that we have before us deals with this issue and offers an account of the institutional efforts made in recent years to strengthen the national capacities required for guaranteeing the conditions of certainty essential for harmonious coexistence, democratic life and development.

The reasons leading to reform of the public security system in Mexico are easily understood. Just four decades ago the country enjoyed a relatively safe environment with low-profile crime, a reality for which the different police forces were designed at that time. Since then crime has evolved and is now characterized by its organizational abilities and access to substantial resources. This means it no longer threatens just people's property, but their very lives. It is obvious that institutions have not changed as quickly as required, nor have they responded to the new crime profile with essential human, technological and operational capacities. The result is clear to everyone and an exhaustive description is unnecessary: suffice to say that the public perceives institutions as ineffective and also mistrusts them.

As is now evident, the transformation of the police system in Mexico requires determination and resources as well as careful planning, such as the development of human capital as an essential principle for strengthening the system. It is precisely the transformation of the human factor that will have the greatest impact on guaranteeing that police actions are professional and remain within the confines of the law. In addition, such changes will lead to the correct use of technological infrastructure and the information and communications tools needed to expand operational and intelligence capacities while facilitating coordinated efforts between those agencies responsible for safeguarding public security.

The system's capacities will, to a great extent, depend on the quality of police officer performance. As this text highlights, by being better prepared, by having more incentives, not only economic but professional, by having a better quality of life, and by receiving benefits such as health services to ensure they feel protected in the face of contingencies, these men and women will help create the necessary conditions to strengthen the government's crime fighting abilities. The top higher education institutions in Mexico are now participating in this effort and will surely continue to do so.

The education of highly trained, responsible and ethical professionals who are aware of society's needs leads to a major commitment on the part of higher education institutions since these professionals understand that in the near future they will be entrusted with the responsibility of guaranteeing public security and social peace for all. When adopting a comprehensive vision of public security and crime prevention it will be necessary for society and its institutions, among them higher education institutions, to assume a share of the responsibility. With contributions from all citizens, no matter what their position, the task that now represents one of the greatest challenges Mexico has ever faced will be completed successfully for the good of the country and all its inhabitants.

THE NEW PUBLIC SECURITY MODEL: THE FEDERAL GOVERNMENT STRATEGY TO TRANSFORM THE PUBLIC SECURITY-SYSTEM

1. The New Public Security Model: the Federal Government Strategy to Transform the Public-Security System

Public security is currently a priority issue of the Mexican Federal Government agenda and one of the most pressing concerns of the citizenry. The process of democratic transition begun by Mexico at the turn of the century, focused public attention and debate on the modernization of political institutions but ignored the urgent need to strengthen public security institutions. While society was undergoing change the country's police forces fell behind and remained steady, something which served to highlight the obsolescence of their operations.

It therefore became necessary to address the pressing challenge of transforming the operational model of police forces in an effort to prevent and fight crime. Deterioration of the police force and a worsening of the underlying causes of increased crime created a problem that needed to be dealt with comprehensively.

This chapter offers a brief overview of certain factors that have influenced the evolution of crime and its growing complexity over the course of recent decades. It also indicates how the operational models used by police forces required structural transformations in order for them to effectively respond to a different kind of criminality.

For this reason the chapter is divided into two sections. The first section broadly analyzes the causes leading to police reform: in other words, the new challenges the police model is required to address and overcome. It also describes how tasks were performed previously and how this prevented public security institutions from developing the necessary human, technological and operational capacities to perform their duties. This resulted in widespread mistrust on the part of the general public and severed the link between society and authorities necessary for the Rule of Law to be viable.

The second section explains the strategic vision used for the design and implementation of a New Public Security Model based on the scientific investigation of crime and intelligence generation for the prevention and combating of crime. Details are offered concerning how this Model, which establishes the bases for redesigning Mexico's public-security system, has served as the starting point for restructuring the Federal Police and offers a reference point for the overhaul of state police forces. The following chapters will analyze each of these central elements separately and in-depth manner.

1.1 Causes Leading to the Transformation of the Federal Police

The transformation of crime phenomena and the deterioration of public-security institutions

Over the past few decades crime has adopted new forms while its operations have become more complex. The institutional framework, originally designed to guarantee public security in Mexico, began to display its shortcomings and limitations for combating a constantly evolving criminal sector.

The 1960s and 1970s

The country had low crime rates in the 1960s and 1970s and during these decades most crimes were low-profile. At the constitutional level the police and police duties were split with municipal preventive police assuming surveillance duties and judicial police being assigned to state and federal public prosecutors. The investigative capacities of the judicial police were fairly rudimentary and the types of crime at the time meant that most cases indicted by public prosecutors were crimes committed *in flagrante*. In other words, there were no political incentives or criminal phenomena that would necessitate development of the investigative or intelligence capacities of the country's police forces.

Social and political stability during this period meant the birth of organized crime, which was largely the result of smuggling activities, went largely unnoticed in Mexico. One of the core elements of the economic model known as "stabilizing development" was protectionism: the country had to be industrialized and in order to achieve these Mexican companies were given protection from foreign competition. Consequently, there were no imports of common use goods (toys, clothing, electrical appliances, etc.) and this led to the emergence of black markets. Foreign merchandise, mainly from the United States, was illegally introduced into the country leading to the creation of networks of corruption and complicity between authorities and smugglers which operated in the areas of customs and of the preventive and judicial police. For its part, the general public saw very little illegal smuggling activity and as a result the buying and selling of smuggled goods became a socially acceptable activity.

By the 1980s protectionist policies had ceased to be relevant and Mexico gradually began to open its borders to foreign trade, making it easier to purchase imported goods outside the black market. Smuggling subsequently lost much of its profitability. Organized crime responded by increasing its participation in more profitable illicit activities such as drug trafficking, which was stimulated by high consumption levels in the United States. At the same time, the economic crisis of the 1980s negatively affected criminal behavior. The public security situation changed radically during this period as kidnappings, aggravated robbery, car theft and other crimes against property emerged as evils that greatly affected the citizenry.

The 1980s

In the 1990s criminal groups exploited new information technologies to expand their operational capacities with organized criminal gangs focusing on the trafficking of drugs, people and arms while coordinating with other organizations to go global. At this time police forces and public prosecutors failed to develop the capacities required to confront these new criminal phenomena.

The 1990s

At the federal level it was clear that in order to detect and dismantle a criminal organization with a hierarchical structure and protective ties with authorities and certain sectors of society, effective police intelligence was required. It was no longer possible to continue using a crime fighting model in which judicial police were required to detect and detain criminals in flagrante. On the contrary, a different type of criminal investigation was now required, one based on information analysis and processing to identify the logistical and financial structures of organized crime, its ties to authorities, its modus operandi and its recruiting mechanisms, among other factors. The judicial police, however, had never developed investigation or intelligence capacities. The preventive police, meanwhile, operated on the basis of an exclusively reactive model and, in some cases, for the containment of disturbances. Mexico lacked a police force capable of tackling criminal phenomena that could no longer be fought through arrests and in flagrante indictments or through simple surveillance and patrolling strategies.

The institutional capacities of the State to perform investigative and intelligence work had been oriented toward questions of social and political control during the preceding decades with the Federal Security Directorate (*Dirección Federal de Seguridad*, DFS), the Investigation Division for the Prevention of Crime (*División de Investigación para la Prevención de la Delincuencia*, DIPD) and the General Directorate of National Security Investigations (*Dirección General de Investigación en Seguridad Nacional*, DGISEN) being just some of the agencies responsible for performing these political intelligence and investigation tasks.

The Center for Investigation and National Security (*Centro de Investigación y Seguridad Nacional*, CISEN) was created in 1989 as a civil intelligence service responsible for information gathering and analysis. In the mid 1990s the CISEN placed its intelligence capacities at the service of public security strategies and operations. This decision produced results as the center helped dismantle several organized crime groups, including certain particularly dangerous groups dedicated to kidnapping. The CISEN was not designed to replace the work of investigative police, however, so its participation was not sufficient to assume the challenges posed by the growth and increasing complexity of criminal activity throughout the country.

Creation of the
Federal Preventive
Police and the
Secretary of Public
Security

The Constitution was amended in 1994 so that states and the federal government could create preventive police forces at the state and federal levels. The Federal Preventive Police (*Policía Federal Preventiva*, PFP) was created in 1999 under the Secretary of the Interior. In 2000 the Secretary of Public Security (*Secretaría de Seguridad Pública Federal*, SSP) was created and the Federal Preventive Police was placed under its command. For the first time an institution was created ex profeso to design and implement public-security policies at the federal level and to coordinate ongoing public security strategies. However, the Federal Preventive Police was unable to consolidate its recruiting and training processes, and neither was it able to replace the reactive model of operation with another based on intelligence that would make it possible to dismantle criminal networks.

The problem of insufficient institutional capacity to confront criminal organizations worsened due to the decentralization of security duties and difficulties within the power structure involving the three levels of government. In 1995, with approval of the General Law that establishes the Bases for Coordination of the National Public Security System, an attempt was made to create national policies based on joint responsible action between authorities of the three levels of government. With this law, federal, state, and municipal institutions were forced to generate and systematize information for the comprehensive analysis of criminal phenomena and to coordinate actions to confront them with a common strategy.

Problems tackling crime and attempts to establish national public security policy

The National Public Security Telecommunications Network was created in 1998 as part of this effort. However, this network was unable to coordinate a homogenous system of information at the national level since individual states and the Federal Government had built telecommunications infrastructure to suit their own specific formats and needs. As a result, it was not possible to establish a single data platform −nor was it possible to standardize protocols and entry formats for data records. The ability to generate criminal intelligence for the entire country using this network was therefore handicapped from the outset.

Creation of the National Public Security Telecommunications Network

On the other hand it was obvious that police forces suffered a deficit of human capital. The minimum level of studies required to perform police work was unsuitable for establishing either a defined hierarchical structure or the different police profiles needed to produce a solid police force[3]. Furthermore, the infrastructure and personnel current at the time were inadequate for providing any form of instruction to police officers: in 2007, according to information from the Superior Auditor of the Federation (*Auditoría Superior de la Federación*, ASF), only one in

Deterioration of Police Responsibilities

---

3. In 1995, for example, of the 58 police training institutions in Mexico only 17 set a minimum educational level as a requisite for becoming a police officer. That is, no previous education was required by two-thirds of police schools. See Gabriela C. Pérez García, *Diagnóstico sobre la seguridad pública en Mexico*, Centro de Análisis e Investigación A.C. (April 2004, p. 21).

four officers had received any form of training[4]. In addition, there were no vetting processes to certify the honesty and moral character of law enforcement officers and no systematic processes serving to guarantee officer profiles suited job requirements.

Deterioration of Police Responsibilities

With little social prestige, inadequate police training and undignified wages and benefits that failed to match the risks and responsibilities of their duties, careers in Mexico's police forces were a vocational choice for persons lacking better opportunities. In many cases officers were people with little education and no expectations for professional growth. They were also on occasion persons of questionable morality and failed to form a true front against increasing crime, at times even joining or serving the interests of criminal gangs.

Obsolescence of Prison Policies

Institutional deterioration also had an impact on a Mexican prison system which had not been considered a fundamental link in the national public security system. The resources earmarked to run prisons were meager and no policies were implemented to make a substantial contribution to rehabilitation. Infrastructure was inadequate for the proper treatment of inmates and custodial staff was not well-trained. To compound these operational problems there were serious problems of overcrowding mainly due to the abuse of the pre-trial detentions system. Prisons were frequently geared toward the inadvertent creation of more dangerous criminals by placing first-time offenders with repeat offenders.

Behavior of Organized Crime and its Links to Criminality

At the beginning of the current Administration the national reality of public security was marked by two closely related trends which required urgent attention. On the one hand there was the growing destructive potential of crime, especially from organized criminal gangs. On the other there was the continuous deterioration and structural weakness of State institutions required to fight new forms of criminality. As far as drug trafficking is concerned, in some parts of the country organized crime was extending its networks of complicity to municipal police and state authorities through bribery, the co-

---

4. Of the police academies in the country, approximately 80% were founded after 1980 and their study programs did not meet authorized criteria or the training needs required for the performance of police duties. Instead, they were governed by the evaluation, experience and capacity of those who headed them.

optation of individuals and intimidation. The operational cells and the logistical and financial structures of these organizations were also used to make inroads into other high-impact crimes such as kidnapping, extortion, armed robbery, human trafficking and arms trafficking.

Organized crime had begun to control, coordinate and manage the criminal underworld and in the process local jurisdiction crimes such as theft began to be connected to organized crime, in the process helping to provide financial support for illegal organized crime structures. This phenomenon runs parallel to the way criminals began to infiltrate more sophisticated areas of crime, no longer merely threatening property but also health, physical integrity and lives. This formed the so-called "pyramid of criminal evolution," which means that criminals begin by committing low-impact crimes such as muggings before moving on to such crimes as burglaries which in turn lead to the committing of high-impact crimes such as kidnappings.

The essential elements of organized crime are therefore the following: the creation of logistical structures necessary to run their illegal activities; the gaining of social acceptance, whether through intimidation or the co-option of persons and communities to prevent the public from reporting crimes and thereby enjoy impunity; institutional protection through the corruption of authorities; and, finally, the control of markets, that is, territorial dominance in order to coordinate and manage local crime, as well as "sell protection" to citizens.

Figure 1. Essential Elements of Organized Crime

To summarize, there was no way to confront this complex criminal phenomenon without a police strategy that abandoned the typically reactive model of *in flagrante* arrests in favor of planning and operating in accordance with a model of intelligence and criminal investigation. This required the design and implementation of a national strategy to transform public-security institutions through the creation of an authentic Federal Police force.

1.2 Key Features of the New Public Security Model in Mexico

The diagnosis was clear: Mexico lacked the police forces necessary to confront criminal phenomena as complex as those described above. In order to develop these institutional capacities it was necessary to design and implement a New Public Security Model.

Key Features
of the New
Public Security
Model

This Model includes, among other key public security features, the systemizing of institutional procedures and structures; the implementation of an operational system that includes fighting and preventing crime through public participation; the professional development of officers from all the country's police forces; and the updating of operational and surveillance systems in Mexico's prisons. These features underpin the process of institutional transformation described in this book. This process required advancing an agenda of legal reforms that would support a New Public Security Model capable of dealing with such fundamental issues as:

New Legal
Framework

- Ending the current organization of police forces whereby preventive policies and crime fighting were kept separate.
- Empowering preventive police to conduct investigations, whether jointly with the Public Prosecutors' Office in the fighting of crime or through the design of strategies to prevent crimes.
- Changing the reactive police control model for a model based on intelligence.
- Systematically generating key criminal information inputs required by police intelligence processes.
- Establishing a system of police development that would be a model for the rest of the country's police forces.
- Modifying the regulatory framework in order to reorganize

the country's prison system through the expansion and effective control of prisons.

Through new institutional design the foundations for police to operate using the basic intelligence cycle were established. This can be summarized using the following four points:

Phases of the Intelligence Basic Cycle

i) *Planning:* police strategy design –to prevent crime or fight crime– starting with objective prioritization and definition, capacities analysis, both technical and operational, and police deployment.
ii) *Gathering:* information related to public security is the primary input for intelligence generation. This stage takes into account the different mechanisms used for collecting intelligence and which range from police reports to open sources, and public complaints to substantive information generated by specialized areas of police investigation.
iii) *Analysis:* at this stage all primary information is processed, the relevant data is selected and value is added by generating technical networks, link networks, geo-crime maps and criminal files on individuals and organizations.
iv) *Exploitation:* intelligence input is produced through the analysis of information used at this stage for the performance of seizure operations, the arrest of criminals, the dismantling of criminal cells or networks and other tasks necessary to guarantee public security and order.

This stage continues with a cyclical process that spirals upward and in which intelligence related to crime phenomena increases as more information is gathered as part of such operations. In this way, the quality of substantive information obtained as part of each intelligence cycle is improved, thereby generating new lines of investigation.

The adoption of this intelligence cycle as a paradigm for police operations permits, for example, the design of strategies for dismantling criminal networks with the starting point being the collection of substantive information on the facts and circumstances (mode, time and place), subjects (name, address, age and other general data) and modus operandi (specific information on the way this criminal group operates).

The information gathered forms the basic input used to open files on suspects; understand liaison networks, beginning with information provided by persons subject to investigation or by victims; and, finally, the generation of geo-crime maps to analyze the spatial-temporal variables of facts related to a crime or a series of crimes.

The usage stage involves the implementation of actions and operations to arrest criminals and dismantle the logistical, operational and financial networks of the criminal organizations they belong to.

These operations in turn allow for new lines of investigation to be generated on the basis of facts related to the organization. As can be demonstrated in the following figure, with each intelligence cycle institutional capacities are strengthened by providing increasingly better information for the fighting of crime, thereby transforming the cycle into a spiral that generates even more knowledge as it develops.

Figure 2. Upwardly Spiraling Intelligence Cycle

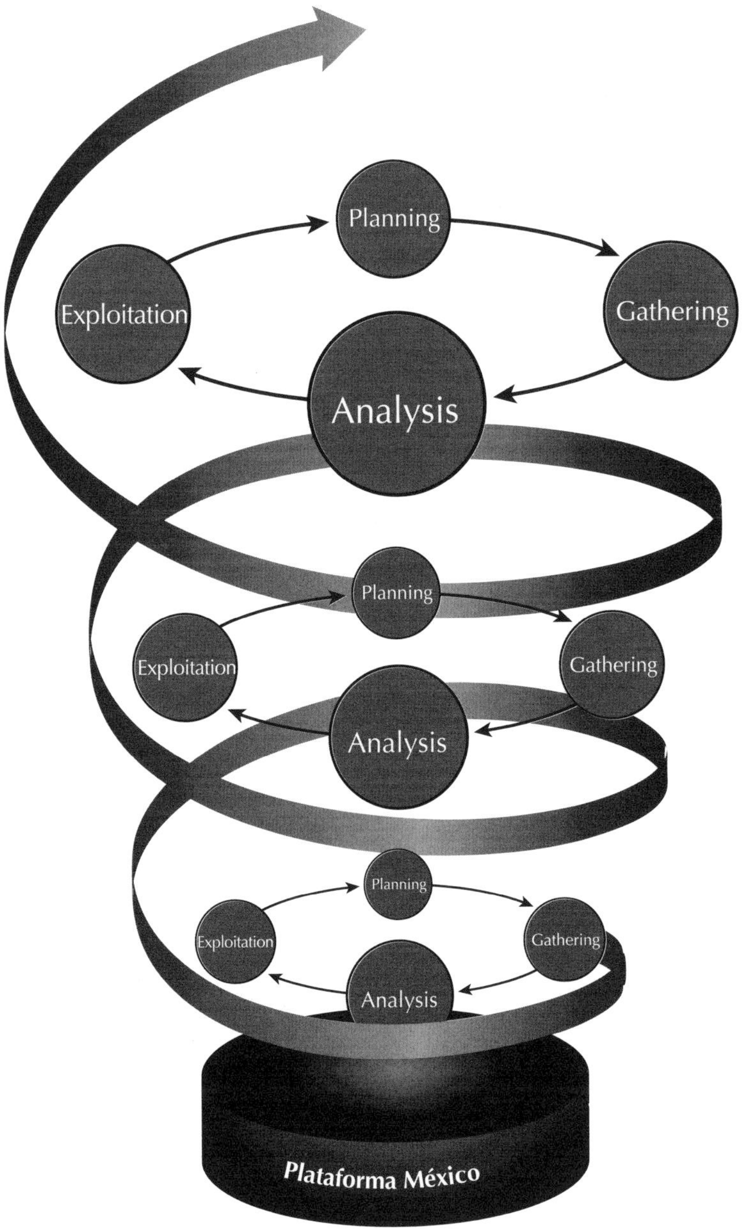

Development of
Human Capital,
Infrastructure
and Technology
for the New
Public Security
Model

At the federal level, and in order to consolidate a police force using the intelligence cycle, the strategy involves two main areas: i) the development of technological capacities and the building of necessary infrastructure, and ii) the development of human skills. Both these areas are closely linked since a professional police force cannot be created without the necessary input and material resources, or without officers enjoying the necessary incentives and training to perform their duties effectively and with a high degree of professionalism.

For this purpose, the key features of the New Public Security Model described in this book seek a balanced relationship between technological and operational resources and human skills. The first of these key features is the establishment of a national network of telecommunications interconnections and databases concentrated into a system called Plataforma Mexico. Given that the police-intelligence cycle uses information as its main input, the first thing that had to be built was a technological platform that would allow information on criminals from the 32 states to be supplied, shared, consulted, analyzed and updated. Furthermore, systemized information protocols and formats had to be developed for the integration of information and the generation of intelligence concerning criminal phenomena. We will analyze Plataforma Mexico in further detail below, outlining what it is and the type of information that can be accessed.

As indicated previously, it would serve no purpose to have databases and the appropriate technology for consultation without human capital trained to use and add value to this information. Restructuring the Federal Police called for designing a Professional Police Career Service, the central element of which is the development of skills and capacities for the different police profiles required to operate as part of the intelligence cycle. A meritocracy system was therefore introduced to control entry, tenure and mobility within the institution, including training, operations and performance criteria for each hierarchical level of the police force, along with entry officer creditability assessments (vetting), tenure, and promotions. An in-depth description of the processes termed the Police Comprehensive Development System (*Sistema Integral de Desarrollo Policial*, SIDEPOL) will be provided later.

Furthermore, an organic/functional restructuring of the police force was conducted, leading to the creation of the new Federal Police. Through this restructuring, the operational capacities of the Federal Police were substantially increased to confront organized crime and other forms of criminality within its area of authority, as well as to ensure better coordination with other police forces and public security institutions. All of this implies, among other things, increased police strength, the creation of new specialized divisions which act as part of the intelligence cycle and the modernization of infrastructure and equipment.

The comprehensive vision guiding operation of the New Public Security Model prioritizes strengthening of the Mexican prison system. The Federal Prison System has been strengthened through actions unmatched in the history of Mexico: the development of infrastructure and the correction of problems that had reduced the capacity and proper functioning of the Federal Prison System for years[5].

In addition, it was essential for the Federal Government to have a professional institution that would, among other things, safeguard the strategic facilities, locations and installations where government institutions operate. Accordingly, the Federal Protection Service (SPF – acronym in Spanish) was created to perform these tasks. It was also necessary to strengthen the supervisory policies of private security companies, taking into account how their role directly impacts public security and crime prevention.

The process of consolidating police reform is long and complex. However, the foundations are now in place. It is now the responsibility of the public to become aware of and evaluate reforms while authorities must guarantee that the police reform process —supported by a national consensus on the urgent need to strengthen public security institutions to fight crime— has the required continuity for consolidation. The possibility of having a professional police force that provides the Mexican Government with the legitimacy and authority required to fight criminality and provide public security depends on the above mentioned factors.

Restructuring the Federal Police

Strengthening the Prison System

Federal Protection Service

---

5. Examples of the Federal Prison System's increased capacity are the expansion of Cefereso No. 4 *Noroeste* in Tepic, Nayarit; repopulation of the Islas Marías Prison Complex, refurbishment of existing structures and the building of new ones; the opening of Cefereso No. 5 in Villa Aldama, Veracruz; the development of prison complexes in Papantla, Veracruz and Guasave, Sinaloa; and the building of eight new federal prison systems commencing with public and private investment plans for the creation of approximately 20,000 new spaces.

THE NEW PUBLIC SECURITY MODEL FOR MEXICO

THE DESIGN OF A NEW PUBLIC SECURITY LEGAL FRAMEWORK

2. The Design of a New Public Security Legal Framework

The legal framework in place prior to the constitutional reform of 2008 no longer responded to Mexican reality and impeded the transformation and modernization of police institutions[6]. Using a comprehensive view, and thanks to a consensus reached by political parties represented in the Congress of the Union and state legislatures, on June 18, 2008, the "Decree for the amendment and addition of diverse provisions of the Political Constitution of the United Mexican States" was approved. This Decree modified the way the role of the State in public security had traditionally been viewed[7].

Several legal provisions were consequently adapted, including: approval of the General Act of the National Public Security System (*Ley General del Sistema Nacional de Seguridad Pública*, LGSNSP) in January 2009, the Federal Police Law (*Ley de la Policía Federal*, LPF) in June 2009, and the "*criminal legislation*

Constitutional Reform of Public Security, Law Enforcement, and Criminal Justice

General Act on the National Public Security System and Federal Police Law

---

6. This diagnosis was shared by the Joint Commissions on Constitutional Matters, Justice, the Interior, Public Security and Legislative Studies of the Senate, which agreed "with the evaluation and analysis of public security and criminal justice matters leading to the proposal by the Federal Executive, as well as the objectives and goals pursued therewith." They shared the idea that in order for the democratic Rule of Law of the State to prevail it was necessary to adapt existing legal and constitutional structures to respond more effectively to crime, but without harming the fundamental rights of the population. See "Reforma constitucional en materia de justicia penal y seguridad pública (proceso legislativo)" in *Cuaderno de apoyo*, Secretaría de Servicios Parlamentarios, Centro de Documentación, Información y Análisis, Dirección de Bibliotecas y de los Sistemas de Información (June 18, 2008).

7. With this decree, amendments and additions were passed to Articles 16, 17, 18, 19, 20, 21 and 22; Paragraphs XXI and XXIII of Article 73; Paragraph VII of Article 115 and Paragraph XIII of Section B of Article 123. Although this amendment included the criminal-justice system, in this text reference is only made to the provisions affecting police operations and that entail their restructuring and reengineering.

miscellanea" published on January 23 of that same year, which were implemented through a series of amendments and additions to the Federal Code of Criminal Proceedings, the Federal Law Against Organized Crime, the Law Establishing Minimum Standards for the Reintegration of Sentenced Persons, the Federal Criminal Code, and the Organizational Law of the Federal Attorney General's Office.

The General Law of the National Public Security System establishes the principles necessary for a new system to coordinate a national crime fighting strategy. With the publication of the Federal Police Law, the Federal Preventive Police was transformed into a force known as the Federal Police and assumed responsibility for preventing and fighting crimes of a federal nature pursuant to constitutional provisions.

These changes have redefined the regulatory framework of pubic security as a function of the three levels of government that includes crime fighting, prevention and investigation, sanctions for administrative offenses, and the social reintegration of inmates. The Constitution did not previously include these features.

The core public security issues covered by amendments to the Constitution can be grouped into the following points:

Key features of Public Security Constitutional Reform

i)   The State was provided with the instruments needed to effectively fight crime. In particular, new powers were given to police for the investigation of crime (Article 21 of the Constitution).

ii) The foundations were laid to hasten the transformation of public security institutions so they could become civil, disciplined and professional in nature, and so that their actions could be governed by the principles of lawfulness, objectivity, efficiency, professionalism, honesty and respect for human rights (Article 21 of the Constitution).

iii) The foundations were redesigned and reinforced in order to coordinate public security institutions (Article 21 of the Constitution)[8].

---

8. Article 5 of the General Law of the Public Security System indicates that public security institutions are "the institutions of the police, Law Enforcement, the Prison System, and agencies responsible for public security at federal, state and municipal levels."

iv) Principles were established for the Mexican prison system to move towards an effective model of social reintegration (Article 18 of the Constitution).

Some of the main innovations of the federal regulatory framework will now be explained. This will begin with analysis of the new regulatory regime for Federal Police investigations and will be followed by a short explanation of how the National Public Security System (*Sistema Nacional de Seguridad Pública*, SNSP) was strengthened to become the agency responsible for effective compliance with coordination mechanisms for the three levels of government.

2.1 Police Investigative Attributions

The Constitution, as has been pointed out, established a strict separation between preventive police and judicial or investigative police. The former were responsible exclusively for implementing crime prevention policies and the latter for crime fighting through their investigation duties. This situation generated two fundamental problems: Firstly, it was responsible for a separation and lack of communication between different police forces. Additionally, relevant information to help develop investigative strategies and design preventive policies was lost. According to this constitutional design, police forces not belonging to the public prosecutors' offices were excluded from a process essential to crime fighting and prevention. This process entailed gathering information, collecting evidence, and exploring lines of investigation.

Problems with the previous separation of police duties

As a consequence of public security legal reform, police are given technical and functional autonomy to investigate crimes through scientific, technical and modern methods that allow them to gather evidence and collect information on groups and individuals, their motives, resources and connections, for the purpose of preventing crimes[9]. In this context, the Federal Police

Virtues of the new institutional design

[9.] Article 2 of the General Law of the Public Security System states that public security "includes the special and general prevention of crime, the investigation to make it effective," as well as "the investigation and pursuit of crimes." Moreover, Article 40 obliges officers of public security institutions to "bring themselves up to date in the use of investigation methods that guarantee the technical and scientific collection of evidence."

can conduct investigations in two ways: in the first investigations are conducted to help prevent criminal acts while in the second investigations are conducted to clarify reported crimes under the auspices of the Federal Public Prosecutor's Office.

Federal Police Duties

These responsibilities have led to wide-ranging changes to activities previously the responsibility of the now extinct Federal Preventive Police. Today, crime prevention no longer refers exclusively to police surveillance of public spaces but also includes "the systematized set of actions and procedures directed toward planning, obtaining, processing and using information, for the sole purpose of avoiding the committing of crimes" (Article 5 of Federal Police Law). In order to do so, this police force can perform the following activities, among others:

i) Regarding investigations to clarify criminal acts, Federal Police can secure, mark, gather, bag and tag, and deliver evidence to the Public Prosecutor's Office in line with applicable provisions. By doing so, in addition to securing the crime scene and the integrity of circumstantial evidence, fingerprints or trace evidence, and of instruments, objects or products of the crime, the Federal Police collects information that may be useful to the Public Prosecutor's Office in order for it to perform its duties (Article 8 of the Federal Police Law).[10]

ii) The General Commissioner of the Federal Police is empowered to authorize -upon agreement with the Secretary of Public Security- covert and infiltration operations[11] (Article 8, Paragraph VII of Federal Police Law) in order to obtain any information serving to prevent or provide warnings of the committing of illicit acts. The Commissioner can also request permission for communications wiretapping from judicial authorities so long as there is sufficient evidence

---

10. With reforms to the Federal Code of Criminal Proceedings published in the Official Gazette of the Federation (Diario Oficial de la Federación, DOF) on January 23, 2009, the rules to be followed by police for the previously described preliminary investigation procedures were modified.

11. These operations refer to the actions of federal police that, through the protection of their true identity, are designed to infiltrate the criminal world and institutional structures to gather, analyze and use the information obtained for the prevention and investigation of crimes.

of the planning of a crime, as stated in Article 51 of Federal Police Law. Examples would include: drug crimes, the corruption of minors, pornography and prostitution, highway robbery, homicides related to organized crime, kidnapping or vehicle theft.[12]

iii) The Federal Police, with prior authorization from a judge, has the authority to request information from companies providing telecommunications and satellite communications systems. Furthermore, the Federal Police can require companies to reveal the location of mobile communications equipment (Article 8, Paragraph XXVIII of Federal Police Law).

iv) Among other prerogatives, the Federal Police can also gather information in public places through any means and instruments necessary to generate preventive intelligence, respecting at all times the right to privacy (Article 8, Paragraph VI of Federal Police Law).

2.2 Establishment of the National Public Security System

The National Public Security System was created in 1995 with the purpose of establishing the necessary synergies between authorities of the three levels of governments to ensure the effective coordination of crime fighting. For the performance of its duties the National Public Security System had an operational technical body called the Executive Secretariat which reported to the Secretary of the Interior until 2001, the year the Secretary of Public Security assumed responsibility. The Executive Secretariat has been responsible for coordinating efforts between the Federal Government and authorities at the state and municipal levels to prevent and fight crime from a technical perspective.

The establishment of the National Public Security System

---

12 Article 16 of the Constitution states that: "only the federal judicial authority, at the request of the federal authority empowered by law or by the Public Prosecutor of the corresponding state, may authorize the wiretapping of any private communications. The competent authority must therefore state the legal grounds and reasons for the request indicating, moreover, the type of wiretap, the suspected individuals, and the duration."

The National Public Security System, however, served more as a mechanism of budgetary resource distribution for public security than as an effective coordination agency. It was unable to encourage suitable plans for the adoption of professional development, vetting, or the dignifying of police duties. In other words, independently of what was established in the legal framework, crime continued to be fought without effective coordination and with police forces in a state of constant deterioration.

For this reason, the National Public Security System was the target of a far-reaching transformation program during the constitutional reform of 2008. In this regard, Article 21 of the Constitution states that the National Public Security System must comply with the following as a minimum:

i)   Regulation of the selection, entry, education, tenure, evaluation, recognition and certification of public security officers. The operation and development of these actions will be the responsibility of the federation, the Federal District, states, and municipalities, within the spheres of their respective powers.

ii) Establishment of criminal and personal databases for public security institutions. No one may join public security institutions if they have not been duly certified and registered in the System.

iii) Formulation of public policies aimed at preventing the committing of crimes.

iv) Community participation for assisting, among other activities, in the processes of evaluating crime prevention policies and also public security institutions.

v)   Federal funding for public security will be assigned to states and municipalities, and will be earmarked exclusively for this purpose.

Pursuant to the foregoing, the purpose of the General Law of the National Public Security System is to regulate the integration, organization and functioning of the System, as well as to establish how duties are assigned and the bases for coordination between the federation, states, the Federal District and municipalities. According to Article 10 of the General Law of the National Public Security System, the National Public Security System is formed by different agencies that permit the coordination of actions for the three levels of government, the maximum authority being the National Public Security Council chaired by the head of the Federal Executive.

Through federal funding for public security the National Public Security System is the agency responsible for guaranteeing that, at the different levels of government, policies and actions are carried out in order to transform and strengthen the public security institutions constituting it[13]. In this regard, in order to guarantee proper management of these resources the plenum of the National Public Security Council may adopt resolutions cancelling or suspending resources assigned to states or municipalities if they breach any of the obligations set forth in this Law. Breaches include: failing to provide, share and systematize public security information; failing to apply procedures and mechanisms for the certification of officers of public security institutions; failing to establish a basic police model other than that determined by the National Public Security Council (Article 144 of the General Law of the National Public Security System).

The planning, budgeting and contributions, as well as exercising, control, evaluation, and auditing of this funding are subject to the Fiscal Coordination Law and the provisions of the

Federal Funding for Public Security

---

13. Article 142 of the General Law of the Public Security System states that: "federal funding for public security, which at the national level is determined by the Federal Budget, shall be distributed to states and municipalities on the basis of the criteria approved by the National Council and for exclusive use for such purposes."

On the other hand, Article 45 of the Fiscal Coordinating Law states that such contributions shall be earmarked exclusively for the recruitment, training, selection, assessment and purging of human resources with public security tasks. Funds shall further be allocated to Public Prosecutors' offices, experts, judicial police or their peers at State and Federal District Attorney General offices, to preventive police or guards at prison centers and misdemeanor centers; for equipment for the judicial police or its equivalents, for experts, for public prosecutors' offices and for preventive police or guards at prisons and youth correction centers; towards establishing and running the National Telecommunications and Computer Network for public security and for the national emergency telephone service; for building, improving or extending facilities, and for justice procurement at prison centers and youth correction centers, as well as for public security corps facilities and training centers; and for following up on and evaluating the aforementioned programs.

General Law of the National Public Security System[14]. For the purposes of transparency and supervision, the Executive Secretary of the National Public Security System can request reports or conduct inspection visits to verify both the legal and timely use of resources, as well as to check advances in compliance with the programs and projects these resources are used to finance.

Executive Secretariat of the National Public Security System

The Executive Secretariat of the National Public Security System was restructured in 2008 to strengthen it as the coordinating agency for the country's public-security institutions. Reform of the Secretary's regulations, which were published that same year, sought to strengthen the scope of its features which include:

i) Proposing policies, guidelines, actions, mechanisms and instruments that strengthen coordination in matters of public security and contribute to their implementation.

ii) Supporting the design and modification of programs in basic training, specialization, promotion and updating of the preventive, judicial, public defense, expert and custodial fields.

iii) Helping with follow-up and evaluation of agreements that, by vote of the Council, are signed with states in matters of public security and in the operation of trusts thereof.

iv) Aiding in the design, development, implementation and administration of the National Public Security Information System.

v) Analyzing bills regarding amendments made to public security laws and regulations submitted to the Council.

vi) Managing and regulating the Public Vehicle Register.

---

14. These measures have been strengthened by modifications to the Federal Criminal Code concerning misuse of public funds since Article 223 states that whomsoever commits such a crime shall be liable to the following sanctions: "When the amount of misappropriated funds or funds used unduly exceeds five hundred times the daily minimum wage in the Federal District at the time of committing the crime, two to fourteen years of prison shall be imposed plus a fine of three hundred to five hundred times the minimum daily wage in the Federal District at the time of committing the crime, and the person shall be barred from holding another public job, position or commission for a period two to fourteen years. When resources involved in the misuse of funds are federal contributions for the purposes of public security, up to one-third more of the fines stated in the preceding paragraphs shall be levied."

The purpose of this restructuring was to give the Executive Secretariat, a technical agency created to coordinate and strengthen the State's capacity to fight crime. In October 2009 it was decided that the Executive Secretariat would be assigned to the Secretary of the Interior, replacing its technical operations leadership in national public security efforts with political leadership –with all of the consequences such a change entails.

***

The fight against crime requires the building of an effective public security legal framework to support a comprehensive policy in this field and contribute to the strengthening, modernization and coordination of institutions comprising the National Public Security System. Notwithstanding pending tasks, Mexico now has laws that lay the foundations for creating police institutions of a civil nature with investigative powers to prevent and fight crime. Specifically, the legal framework has been strengthened, transforming the Federal Police into a professional and modern police force with new and better operational, human and technological capacities for the fighting of crime. These changes have transformed the Federal Police into a national benchmark for police reform.

Conclusions

THE NE
PUBLIC
SECURI
MODEL
FOI
MEXICO

DEVELOPMENT OF
TECHNOLOGICAL
INFRASTRUCTURE
FOR POLICE
INTELLIGENCE

3. Development of Technological Infrastructure for Police Intelligence

Transforming public security in Mexico required modernization of the tools police forces use to fight crime. The transition from a reactive model to a model favoring prevention and the scientific investigation of crime made it necessary to establish the technological infrastructure necessary for the consultation of substantive information concerning crime in real time.

With the creation of the National Public Security System a number of efforts were made to create databases on crime, criminals, and police, but these efforts produced very limited results. Relevant information for generating police intelligence was disorganized, was not shared by institutions, or simply did not exist. It was therefore essential to develop police intelligence that contributed, among other things, to understanding criminal networks and their *modus operandi*. Police forces lacked the inputs and the technological infrastructure to operate according to this new model.

For this reason, during the current administration the National Interconnection Network known as Plataforma Mexico was designed and brought into operation. This is a technological project that for the first time in Mexico allows the three levels of government to exchange information on public security, thereby acquiring the basic inputs allowing them to develop police intelligence to better fight crime.

Below we will explain the system's relevance in integrating useful information to help generate intelligence. Second, a description is provided of the technological design, databases, and main applications of Plataforma Mexico. Subsequently, reference will be made to the Federal Police Intelligence Center (*Centro de Inteligencia de la Policía Federal*, CIPF), a key element in the operation of Plataforma Mexico. Emphasis is placed on the abilities of this tool to strengthen cooperation with other countries for the exchange of police information.

Use of technology in crime prevention

3.1 Plataforma Mexico: The Technological Expression of the New Public Security Model

Plataforma Mexico is a National Interconnection Network which makes the creation of the Unified Criminal Information System (*Sistema Único de Información Criminal*, SUIC) possible. The network is the infrastructure that permits communication and the exchange of information between security institutions and other government agencies. In turn, the Unified Criminal Information System collects and concentrates records in databases and includes a variety of applications and analytical tools for the generation of intelligence.

The design and characteristics of Plataforma Mexico make it possible to:

- Consolidate databases on national criminal phenomena
- Authorize procedures for the use of public security information
- Implement systems for maintaining and storing the databases forming part of the Unified Criminal Information System
- Serve as liaison between agencies entrusted with law enforcement and with public security organizations throughout the country
- Generate operational intelligence

To launch Plataforma Mexico it was necessary to establish a legal framework as well as commitments and agreements with agencies forming the National Public Security System. The goal was for all three levels of government to exchange useful information on public security and law enforcement. During the Twenty-First Session of the National Public Security Council, encouragement was given and agreements reached so that Plataforma Mexico start-up would be achieved through two courses of action: i) the technological infrastructure program would be updated and the National Interconnection Network strengthened, and ii) the Unified Criminal Information System would function as one of the National Information System's most important components.

Similarly, one of the most important requirements to ensure the project functioned was the toughening of laws to force authorities from the different levels of government to provide reliable and useful information for fighting crime. At present, Article 109 of the General Law of the National Public Security System states that the federation, states, Federal District and municipalities shall supply, exchange, systematize, consult, analyze and update the public security information generated daily by means of the respective technological systems and instruments, thereby having real-time data for designing crime fighting programs and policies. Furthermore, Article 110 states that one duty of officers serving in the National Public Security System is to exchange the information they generate –something made possible today by the development of Plataforma Mexico which is part of the Secretary of Public Security.[15]

In order to guarantee correct operation of the National Information System, Article 111 of the General Law of the National Public Security System states that the three levels of government have the responsibility to ensure compatibility between their local network telecommunications services and the following Plataforma Mexico systems and databases.

Plataforma Mexico Systems and Databases

i) *Unified Criminal Information System (SUIC)*: this System is formed by information generated by law enforcement institutions and police institutions concerning persons who have been indicted, prosecuted or sentenced. Information must include their criminal profile, means of identification, resources and *modus operandi*, arrest warrants, criminal proceedings, and sentencing and sentence enforcement. It also includes the National Prison Information System (*Sistema Nacional de Información Penitenciario*, SNIP), which for the first time contains inmate files for the prison systems of the three levels of government.

ii) *Administrative Register of Detentions*: this Register is comprised of reports submitted by police officers in the form of Systemized Police Reports (*Informes Policiales Homologados*, IPH). This Register is updated with information from law enforcement institutions once the detainee is at their

---

15. To ensure compliance with this obligation, the Law considers monetary and criminal sanctions as well as the barring and disqualification of any person who deceitfully, illegally or continually abstains from providing the information they are compelled to provide in the terms stated.

disposal (Articles 112-116 of the General Law of the National Public Security System).[16]

iii) *National Register of Public Security Personnel (Police Kardex)*: this Register includes information that helps identify and locate members of public security institutions, such as fingerprints, photographs, education and service backgrounds, among other factors.

iv) *National Weapons and Equipment Register*: authorities with jurisdiction at the three levels of government update this Register, which includes vehicles, weapons and ammunition assigned by agencies to public servants in the performance of their duties.

Finally, as part of the Collaboration and Access to Information Model the Permanent Information Commission of the National Public Security Council approved criteria for providing, systemizing and updating information on Plataforma Mexico, pursuant to the following guidelines:

Guidelines:

- Connectivity to Plataforma Mexico
- Logical Security of Plataforma Mexico
- System User Administration
- Systemized Police Report
- National Register of Public Security Personnel
- Register of Stolen and Recovered Vehicles
- National Register of Weapons and Equipment
- Drivers Licenses Register
- Fingerprint Register
- System of Identification of Persons through Voice Analysis
- System of Automatic Recognition of Vehicle License Plate Numbers

---

16. Once the preliminary investigation or file is opened, Public Prosecutor authorities notify the National Information Center on-line and in real time –using the Unified Criminal Information System and referring to Systematized Police Reports– that the detainees or persons presented are at their disposal. The aforementioned Center is notified of the legal situation of the suspect and receives data to help identify suspects. If an arrest warrant or notice to appear before a judge is issued, the Center provides information on the person(s) for whom the warrant was issued and the crime(s) they are charged with (Articles 18 and 20 of the *Policies for Furnishing, Exchanging, Systematizing and Updating Information on Public Security Generated by Public Security Institutions of the three levels of Government* issued by the Permanent Information Commission on October 2, 2009.)

3.1.1 Building the Plataforma Mexico Network

One of the major challenges when launching the New Public Security Model was consolidating Plataforma Mexico as a robust and flexible network with high levels of security and availability, and with standardized technology throughout the country. It required an adequate technological infrastructure to support the operation of a professional and modern police force.

The first stage of the project consisted of setting up a new National Interconnection Network capable of accessing databases and transferring public security and law enforcement records for the entire country. Additionally, it had to be capable of transmitting voice recordings, data and images in real time.[17] Thanks to a combination of factors including the technology used and devices that automatically distribute information traffic, the network was designed to generate up to 15,000 simultaneous connections per second and 40 million protected information transmissions. This helps prevent saturation of the system and optimizes the layered performance and design of the network and its applications.

Due to its scalable design, Plataforma Mexico is able to integrate new applications gradually and boost its capacities without risking either its optimal performance or the strict levels of security it employs to protect the information stored.[18] Another major strength of this network is its system redundancy. Redundancy provides the necessary technological back-up to function without interruption and to send information by other means should any of its components fail.[19]

The network's technological characteristics make it possible to integrate more thorough security measures. Plataforma Mexico directly manages, on the one hand, technological padlocks to

---

17. The network was built using Internet-Protocol-Multiprotocol Label Switching (IP-MPLS). This Protocol permits running and designing a network in a more simplified form and provides the network with greater scalability and operational capacity.

18. One example is that the bandwidth supporting Plataforma Mexico network can be expanded to 30 MB to avoid saturation.

19. When a non-redundant system is available only one channel is used for the sending of information. A system such as this shuts down if any of the services supplying it fail, thereby preventing a continued and reliable service.

block the entry of unauthorized external users, and on the other, user authentication to access information in accordance with one of its three levels of complexity:

i) *Police operations*: this level of information provides access to police reports, criminal inquiries, and arrest records, and is the basic level of information used by police officers to perform their daily duties.

ii) *Investigation and analysis*: this is the mid-level of information and provides access to cases, investigations, criminal records, and criminal and reference inquiries. This tool is used by investigative police forces.

iii) *Intelligence information*: this is the top level of information —and also the most restricted. It provides access to information on operational intelligence, data correlation and cross-referencing, control boards, and crime maps.

Without adversely affecting the network's strict security levels, police forces can check connections and search for information in real time to strengthen their operational capacities. For example, the network's design allows for the use of data-sharing wireless devices and this makes it possible to check information stored in databases from any point in the country using a laptop, mobile phone, radio or PDA. This illustrates the tool´s potential for the daily operations of the nation's police forces.

Plataforma Mexico
Technological
Security Padlocks

One of the most important contributions of the new network is the updating of state Control, Command, Communications and Computation Centers (C4), and those referred to as sub-C4s which are converted into Nodes and Sub-Nodes of Telecommunication Interconnection (NIT and SUBNIT, respectively). This has helped standardize technology throughout Mexico and as a result state and public security and law enforcement institutions can now exchange information and communicate in real time.[20]

---

20. As of the first quarter of 2011, Plataforma Mexico systems and applications had already been installed at the 32 Attorney General Offices, the 32 Secretaries of Public Security, as well as at more than 30 Finance Secretaries and 34 prison centers. At the municipal level they had already been installed at 195 municipalities aided by the Subsidy for Municipal Security (Subsidio para la Seguridad Municipal, Subsemun). In each case the Secretary of Public Security has provided training for use of the Plataforma Mexico.

With Plataforma Mexico a significant step has been taken to more effectively coordinate the daily operations of Mexico's public security institutions through interaction with the Federal Police Command Center located in Mexico City.

3.1.2 Databases Forming the Unified Criminal Information System

While an efficient network was being built to transfer information using advanced security measures, work was also underway to integrate and bolster databases created by the Federal Government and state institutions. The chart below describes the databases in the Unified Criminal Information System, in addition to showing the number of records contained in each database.

Databases forming the Unified Criminal Information System

Chart 1. Databases in the Unified Criminal Information System and Total Number of Records at Q1, 2011.

Database Name	Content	Records
Biometrics	Genetic markers; the automated fingerprint identification system; the automated biometric voice-identification system; the facial-recognition system (including a list of the most-wanted criminals); and a system of ballistic correlation for public and private security personnel, military and naval personnel, inmates of federal, state and municipal prisons; suspects registered with state Attorney General Offices and the Federal Attorney General's Office, as well as letters concerning a person's past criminal conduct issued by certain states.	6,847,445
Drivers Licenses	All drivers licenses in the country.	51,765,289
Stolen or Recovered Vehicles	Reports on stolen and recovered vehicles across the country.	1,984,398

Public Vehicle Register (Repuve)	Contains vehicle identification numbers, proof of registration, and electronic identification.	30,908,419
Federal and Local Court Orders	Centralizes court orders, such as state and federal warrants for arrest, re-arrest and subpoenas	2,717,831
Indicted, Prosecuted and Sentenced Individuals	Includes criminal records, means of identification, resources and modus operandi.	1,203,148
Open Sources	Information from printed or audiovisual mass media communication and from diverse companies and non-media sources.	295,662,894
Weapons	Contains the registration number, make, model, caliber, serial number and other information necessary for the identification of weapons.	646,970
Mexicans Serving Sentences Abroad	Information on persons incarcerated in other countries: personal information, crime profile and means of identification.	195,365
Advance Passenger Information System (APIS)	Airline registers of persons arriving in Mexico via international airports that make immediate alerts possible.	17,589,426
Integral System of Migratory Operation (SIOM)	Data on migration controls and flows, undocumented migrants repatriated and held, among others.	7,915,281
Coordinating Office of Insured Risks (OCRA)	Insurance companies vehicle register.	699,747
Total		**418,136,213**

*At present databases are still being integrated into the System, which is scalable.

3.1.3 Plataforma Mexico Applications

The automatic search engines of Plataforma Mexico are decisive tools in police intelligence generation. With these, when coincidental factors are found (data such as names, vehicle license plates, etc.) in available criminal records, a notification known as an "alert" is automatically sent to the corresponding authority, whether federal, state or municipal. This step is the system's cornerstone since it constantly and automatically links new information with existing data in real time to generate new intelligence products. Applications of the Unified Criminal Information System include:

i)   *Systemized Police Report (IPH)*: creates a record of crime scene facts related to any police involvement. Systemized Police Reports should include, among other data, the name and alias of the detainee, if applicable, as well as their physical description, fingerprints, anthropometric identification, address, date of birth, marital status, education and occupation; motive; the general circumstances, location and time when the arrest was made, the place the person was detained and where they were transferred.

The Systemized Police Report also generates information that provides data on weapons, persons, vehicles and objects for classification. It additionally determines the precise location of a crime scene cartographically; automatically provides cross-referred information and generates statistics, geo-crime maps and intelligence products. If the information reported by police matches the Unified Criminal Information System databases, alerts are sent automatically to the Federal Police Command Center or the corresponding local agency.

At present, for the System's start-up phase, there are a total of 537,133 Systemized Federal Police Reports and 1,792,713 reports from States.

ii) *The Police Kardex*: an information system with a record for each police officer in Mexico's security corps. It provides detailed information on their backgrounds and has seven modules containing personal and professional information, as demonstrated in the following chart:

Chart 2. Police Kardex Information

Module	Information Included
General Information	Address, fingerprints, DNA record, voice record, graphology, physical description (detailed physical features, especially the face), results of vetting, and socio-economic information.
Work Experience	Current position, experience in the area of public security, previous jobs, services, commissions, and leave time.
Service and Equipment	Duties performed as well as vehicles, side arms, shoulder weapons, and radio-communications used at work.
Academic Development	Formal education, languages, public-security training and teaching.
Discipline and Police Justice	Merits (stimuli and promotions) and demerits (corrective disciplinary actions and administrative sanctions) accumulated during an officer's police career.
Benefits	Housing credit and legal assistance insurance.
Service Termination	Explicit concerning whether termination was due to demerits, was voluntary (resignation or voluntary withdrawal), or for reasons of retirement, disability or death.

Consulting the Police Kardex will help ensure that officers dismissed from any public security institution for crimes or infractions do not join another police force in a different state. Additionally, it will prevent the entry, tenure and promotion of police officers if they lack the required capacities. At present, there are a total of 1,334,120 records available in the Police Kardex. [21]

---

21. As of the first quarter of 2011, 31 states had uploaded over 80% of police officer records to the Kardex. However, the Federal District advanced only 76.5%. There is information from 195 municipalities benefitted by Subsemun. Total Kardex records refer to persons who have been police officers and those on active duty.

iii) *Criminal Record*: an application that permits the systemization of information covering personal data, identification, activities and criminal events the person has been involved in as a suspect or probable culprit. At present a total of 514,403 criminal records are stored.

iv) *Case Modules*: these enable the integration of police investigation information, from network analysis as well as field work. This Module classifies and standardizes information about complaints, preliminary investigations, persons, vehicles, weapons, real estate, and communication devices involved in the committing of crimes –and also in the prevention of crimes. It also includes analytical tools such as liaison networks and technical networks, crime geo-referencing, and statistical reports. The Case Module includes a section for each of the more than 50 crimes classified as federal. At present, the module contains 5,075 cases under investigation.[22]

v) *Private Security Module*: this Module contains a Unified Database of Private Security Companies in Mexico. It provides and constantly updates records and databases related to private security service providers, their personnel, infrastructure and equipment. It is now possible to access up-to-date information on these services not only for the purpose of regulating the sector but also for public security tasks and duties.

vi) *National Prison Information System* (Sistema Nacional de Información Penitenciaria, *SNIP*): a nationwide information system that centralizes and standardizes administration of Prevention and Social Reintegration Centers. It is formed by the following modules: the Indicted and Sentenced Persons Registry System, the Federal Prisons System, the Inmates and their Families Attention Unit Control System, the National Sentenced Persons Archive System, Prison Infrastructure, Benefit Control, the Sentenced Population

---

22. As of the first quarter of 2011, 32 state Attorney General Offices had installed case modules. However, only 30 of them are in operation since the Quintana Roo Attorney General's Office does not have staff able to upload information and the Tlaxcala Attorney General's Office has not registered any events since 2010.

on Parole Control and Surveillance System, National and International Transfers, and the Prison Information Exchange System.

As far as the Indicted and Sentenced Persons Register System is concerned, the National Prison Information System establishes connectivity conditions for the existing 429 prison centers so that information can flow as needed for the centers' daily operations and for criminal investigations. At present, 128 of these centers are connected.

vii) *Operational Management System* (Sistema de Gestión Operativa, *SGO*): thanks to the Operational Management System information held in Unified Criminal Information System applications and databases can be used to plan operational deployments and respond to calls for support made by state and municipal officers in the different areas of the Federal Police and other agencies. The Operational Management System also permits each level of government to follow up on individual police officers and the weaponry and vehicles at their disposal.

Given the importance of the system's cartography, a Geographical Information System was included. This was built in collaboration with leading institutions in the field and uses the latest technology (high-precision software, aerial photographs, photogrammetry, photo interpretation, satellite imaging and new methodologies for the making of geographical maps). This function allows for the creation of "thematic crime maps" which pinpoint where, and describe how and indicate what types of crimes are being committed and how crime spreads geographically. Information is provided concerning criminal patterns and this proves invaluable when determining the location and method for performing operations.

viii) *On-Line Collaboration System*: in order to facilitate and encourage collaboration between the Federal Government and state and municipal governments, a technological tool is included in the Unified Criminal Information System which allows police officers to communicate in real time and exchange and obtain useful information for the arrest of criminal suspects and coordination of police force deployment.

ix) *Public Complaints Systems*: at present there are two systems for public complaints: Emergency and Anonymous Complaints Call Centers (*Centro de Atención de Emergencias y Denuncia Anónima*, CAEDA) and the National Center for Citizen Attention (*Centro Nacional de Atención Ciudadana*, CNAC).

CAEDA centers were created to receive reports from the public via 066 and 089 telephone numbers and help coordinate police forces at the three levels of government to deal with crime and perform civil protection duties. These Centers are permanently linked to the Unified Criminal Information System for the forwarding of information. In the case of an alert, intelligence officers respond to anonymous complaints by deploying response forces or by opening a corresponding investigation.

For its part, the National Center for Citizen Attention is run by the Federal Police and has a computer system that receives complaints about any illegal act via the 088 telephone number, its website (www.ssp.gob.mx) or cell-phone text messaging (90089); the goal is to integrate all information generated by states, the Federal District and municipalities.

The two key features of the Public Complaints System are detailed complaints geo-referencing by crime and the generation of statistics. These features help in the design of police actions and crime prevention strategies.

3.2 Federal Police Intelligence Center

The Federal Police Intelligence Center (*Centro de Inteligencia de la Policía Federal*, CIPF) is the nerve center of the Plataforma Mexico Network and houses the tools for exploiting information in Unified Criminal Information System databases for the generation of intelligence products. In addition, cutting-edge technology used to support operations is designed to guarantee public security and combat crime.

The Federal Police Intelligence Center incorporates best practices from around the world and meets the most rigorous security standards for building and configuring data centers. As previously mentioned the Federal Police Intelligence Center can perform 15,000 transactions per second and provides instant access to its online databases. To put this into perspective, this number of operations is equivalent to half the total banking transactions carried out in the entire United States during an equivalent time period.

The Federal Police Intelligence Center also houses a National Command Room equipped with the instruments and security needed to respond to any contingency arising throughout the country. These contingencies may be the result of human factors or natural disasters. The Federal Police Intelligence Center is divided into four areas:

i) *Operations Area*: this area performs special operations in support of the different Federal Police Divisions through the use of a variety of technologies, such as transmissions, information reception via satellite, or tracking and following unidentified flights with a radar system, among others.

ii) *Strategic Infrastructure Area*: this area, through collaboration protocols with institutions such as *Petróleos Mexicanos* (Pemex), the *Comisión Federal de Electricidad* (CFE) and the *Comisión Nacional del Agua* (Conagua), is entrusted with preventing acts of sabotage and/or terrorism targeting the facilities of the aforementioned agencies through the use of early-warning systems.

iii) *National Alert Area*: the primary function of this area is to give advance warning of natural disasters or events that might place the population at risk. For this purpose a National Risks Atlas has been compiled and mathematical models have been developed so that through the location of hospitals, accommodation and infrastructure where these events occur, the affected areas can be sealed off and evacuations efficiently planned.

iv) *Security Area*: the usefulness of this area is demonstrated through the Unit for the Coordination and Exchange of Police Information (*Unidad de la Coordinación e Intercambio de Información Policial*, UCIIP) which links local and Federal governmental efforts in the areas of analysis of substantive information and fieldwork for the purpose of creating authorized data systems to help investigate and solve crimes.

The Federal Police Intelligence Center has modern mechanisms to guarantee maximum levels of security and includes areas dedicated to network operation supervision and service infrastructure security to ensure the continuous functioning of operations performed at the Center.

The challenge now is for states to move in a similar direction. Plataforma Mexico currently offers a subsidy so that states can maintain storage capacity, data processing, and interaction with all applications in the area of public security. What is needed now is for states to develop the human skills needed to take full advantage of the systems included in Plataforma Mexico for the generation of operational intelligence for fighting crime.

3.3 International Cooperation for Intelligence Exchange

Given the challenge presented by organized crime and international criminal activities, it became essential to increase Mexican government capacities through collaboration with other countries. During the current Administration institutional links have been fostered with other countries to work together and exchange information in the area of public security. Plataforma Mexico has facilitated actions and measures contributing to this cooperation strategy with other countries and international organizations by guaranteeing the timely exchange of information and intelligence. Thanks to a collaborative agreement signed in 2008 with Interpol, Plataforma Mexico is now connected to the Global Police Communications System, making Mexico one of the first countries to exchange and automatically feed its databases with information from this international organization.

In addition, cooperative agreements have been established with a number of countries. One example is the strengthening of the public security relationship with the United States of America through the signing of agreements for the exchange of information and operational collaboration.[23] Similarly, when

International Cooperation Networks for Crime Fighting

---

23. In February 2010 the Secretary of Public Security and the United States Department of Homeland Security (DHS) issued a joint declaration of cooperation to reinforce the border between the two countries and combat transnational threats, beginning with the exchange of information and intelligence.

considering the common interests and issues characterizing the relationship between Mexico and other Latin American countries, it was considered essential to foster collaboration with the region's police forces and police intelligence organizations. The following actions were consequently taken:

i)   Adoption of the Security Strategy for Central America and Mexico (SICA-Mexico Dialogue), which agreed that the core issues to be dealt with included drug trafficking, human trafficking, money laundering, terrorism, and illegal arms trafficking. It was agreed that an exchange of information was fundamental in order to generate intelligence.[24]

ii) Inclusion of the Secretary of Public Security in the Latin American and Caribbean Police Intelligence Community (CLACIP) formed by 27 intelligence agencies from 25 countries for the purpose of combating the diverse activities of transnational organized crime in the region through the exchange of information, intelligence and experience, along with the design of coordinated strategies. It should be pointed out that the Secretary of Public Security assumed the CLACIP chairmanship for the period 2009-2011.

iii) Adoption of the document "Commitment to Public Security in the Americas" within the framework of the Inaugural Meeting of Public Security Ministers of the Americas (MISPA), held in Mexico, including actions leading to an increased exchange of substantive information to combat transnational crime.[25]

iv) In addition, Mexico presided over the International Drug Enforcement Conference (IDEC), held in April 2011, thanks to the efforts of the Secretary of Public Security.

---

24. The governments Mexico has adopted this strategy with are: Belize, Costa Rica, El Salvador, Guatemala, Honduras, Nicaragua and Panama. Another of the core issues is cooperation in the areas of prevention, education, and training.

25. Countries attending this meeting, held jointly with the Organization of American States (OAS) in October 2008, were Antigua and Barbados, Argentina, the Bahamas, Belize, Bolivia, Brazil, Canada, Chile, Colombia, Costa Rica, Dominica, the Dominican Republic, Ecuador, El Salvador, Guatemala, Guyana, Haiti, Honduras, Jamaica, Mexico, Nicaragua, Panama, Paraguay, Peru, Saint Kitts and Nevis.

An agenda of cooperation has been advanced with Europe and Asia with the fundamental purpose of taking advantage of best practices in information technology and intelligence to contribute both to greater tactical development of the Federal Police and the fighting of transnational crime.[26] At the same time, institutional links were furthered in order to work directly with public security institutions in strategic countries and regions for the formation of a common front against transnational crime. Offices were subsequently opened in the United States of America, Guatemala, Colombia and Spain. Greater collaboration is being achieved as a result of these links, mainly between the operational areas of the Federal Police and the security agencies of these countries to follow up on joint investigations and strengthen bilateral and regional cooperation agendas.

Cooperation and Institutional Ties with Europe and Asia

***

Establishment of Plataforma Mexico has not only helped resolve problems that hindered the coordination of information exchange and usage between agencies responsible for public security and law enforcement at the three levels of government, it has also created the technological capacities to compile and analyze information in real time, leading to the increasingly solid generation of intelligence products. In addition to overcoming the information obsolescence previously faced by police, through the development of this tool Mexico has acquired the technological capacities to make the transition from a reactive police model to a model based on the use of criminal information and intelligence.

Conclusions

---

26. To meet these goals and expand Mexico's international relations in the area of security, bilateral working agendas were established for the first time with Japan, China, South Korea, Israel, Germany, Spain, Italy, the United Kingdom, the Netherlands, Russia, Belgium and the Czech Republic.

THE NEW PUBLIC SECURITY MODEL FOR MEXICO

POLICE COMPREHENSIVE DEVELOPMENT SYSTEM

4. Police Comprehensive Development System

Implementing the New Public Security Model not only required developing technological capacities and databases for the generation of police intelligence, it also required appropriate human resources to operate and exploit this technology and information. The Police Comprehensive Development System (*Sistema Integral de Desarrollo Policial*, SIDEPOL)[27] was designed precisely for this purpose and has the following objectives:

Police Comprehensive Development System

Objectives of the Police Comprehensive Development System
- Promote institutional development.
- Guarantee job stability and equal opportunities for police force officers.
- Raise the level of professional development.
- Foster a vocation of service and a sense of belonging.

This System has four key features: the Professional Police Career Service –one of its elements being Credibility Assessment (Vetting) – the Professional Development Master Program; the Disciplinary Regime; and the Complementary Social Security System. Each feature of the Police Comprehensive Development System will be analyzed below and the actions taken by Federal Police to implement these features will be described.

Key Features of the Police Comprehensive Development System

---

27. As its legal foundation, the Police Comprehensive Development System uses the General Law of the National Public Security System which establishes, in Article 72, a system of police development incorporating a comprehensive set of duly structured and linked rules and structures that encompass the career of Police Officer, professional development plans, certification, and the disciplinary regime for police force officers. It also sets forth the obligation of police forces to implement the System to guarantee the development of officers.

4.1 Professional Police Career Service

The first feature of the Police Comprehensive Development System is the Professional Police Career Service, which is a compulsory and permanent subsystem that establishes the processes for recruitment, selection, entry, professional development, certification, assimilation, tenure, promotion, stimuli, decoration and, ultimately, conclusion of officer service in the force.[28]

The first step in creating the Professional Police Career Service was to define the structure to be applied nationwide as well as the categories and hierarchies, duties, responsibilities and profiles required to ensure the optimum performance of police duties.

Duties in police force operational areas:

- Investigation: carried out through homogeneous systems for the gathering, classification, recording, analysis, evaluation and use of information.

- Prevention: through the use of inspection and surveillance procedures.

- Response: through actions that guarantee, maintain and reestablish public order and peace.

The areas of Investigation, Prevention and Response are based on a structure featuring four categories with thirteen hierarchical levels of command and responsibility, as shown in the following chart:

---

28. On this topic, see Article 79 of the General Law of the National Public Security System which establishes Police Career goals.

Chart 3: Police Careers by Rank, Academic Level and Hierarchical Level

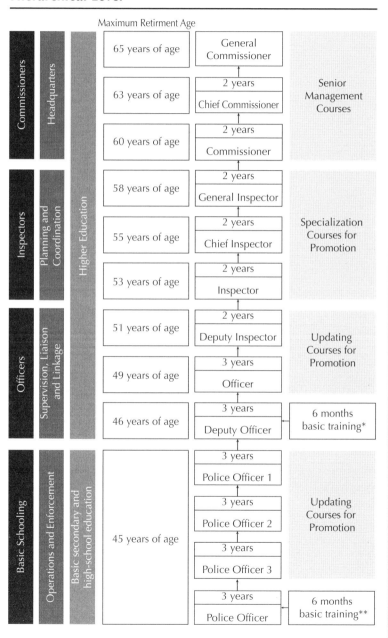

Maximum Retirement Age

Commissioners	Headquarters	Higher Education	65 years of age	General Commissioner	Senior Management Courses
			63 years of age	2 years / Chief Commissioner	
			60 years of age	2 years / Commissioner	
Inspectors	Planning and Coordination		58 years of age	2 years / General Inspector	Specialization Courses for Promotion
			55 years of age	2 years / Chief Inspector	
			53 years of age	2 years / Inspector	
Officers	Supervision, Liaison and Linkage		51 years of age	2 years / Deputy Inspector	Updating Courses for Promotion
			49 years of age	3 years / Officer	
			46 years of age	3 years / Deputy Officer	6 months basic training*
Basic Schooling	Operations and Enforcement	Basic secondary and high-school education	45 years of age	3 years / Police Officer 1	Updating Courses for Promotion
				3 years / Police Officer 2	
				3 years / Police Officer 3	
				3 years / Police Officer	6 months basic training**

* Candidates enter at the bachelor degree level
** Candidates enter at the secondary or high-school level

Police Training
Process

The second step in developing the Professional Police Career Service was to establish the criteria and protocols for each process. Academic levels and specific training had to be determined for each operational category and hierarchical level, along with level of entry into the police force, in accordance with the candidate's level of schooling. Similarly, basic training processes for candidates were defined, in addition to continuous police officer training and education and the retirement ages for each category.

These criteria and protocols further specify the minimum requirements a candidate must meet in order to be recruited, such as not having been given a final sentence for intentional crimes or not being involved in a criminal trial. Candidates must also prove their levels of educational achievement and pass the vetting process. Additionally, selection processes are defined; periodic assessments are applied to ensure tenure; mechanisms for promotion, merits, recognition, stimuli and rewards are provided; and the possible causes for dismissal from the police force are described. From the moment of their entry, officers are fully aware of the requirements and conditions for professional development. Professional Police Career Service processes and objectives are described in the following chart:

Process	Objective
Recruitment	Establish the requirements for acceptance by the Police.
Selection	Determine whether candidates meet the required profile through testing and assessment in accordance with the National Vetting Model and specific testing protocols approved by the National Public Security Council.
Certification	Identify risk factors that may interfere with, affect or endanger the performance of police duties by means of periodic assessments established by the corresponding Vetting Center.

---

29. There are two hierarchical levels for candidate entry in accordance with their educational level: a) police officer, which requires the completion of secondary or high-school studies; b) deputy officer, which requires completion of a Bachelor's degree. Both entry levels are followed by a basic six-month training period.

Entry	Formalize the entry of police officers by issuing an official designation that establishes rights, obligations and prohibitions.
Basic Training	Prepare candidates through educational processes designed to impart knowledge and develop abilities, skills and aptitudes.
Continuous Training	Strengthen police officer abilities, skills and aptitudes in all categories and hierarchies by updating their knowledge in order to improve professional performance.
Tenure	Evaluate police officer performance and professional productivity on the basis of how they fulfill their duties and pass vetting.
Assimilation	Regulate the entry of personnel with military training and experience, along with personnel from other police forces or other fields –academic or business– into the ranks of the country's public security secretaries based on the general criteria guiding the revalidation of academic histories and work experience.
Mobility	Set police officer requirements and training paths for those wanting to change their field of specialization or institution for any of the three levels of government, either horizontally or vertically.
Promotions	Determine the corresponding procedures for promoting police officers to the next rank in the hierarchical order.
Termination	Define and establish the options police officers have when reaching the end of their active career and, if applicable, dismiss them on the basis of legally established causes.ine and establish the options police officers have when reaching the end of their active career and, if applicable, dismiss them on the basis of legally established causes.
Recognition, Stimuli and Rewards	Encourage quality, effectiveness and loyalty, and increase the possibilities for promotion among active police officers through recognition of merit.

4.1.1 Credibility Assessment (Vetting)

An essential tool of the Professional Police Career Service is creditability assessment (vetting), which ensures that anyone aspiring to join a police department fits the profile for the performance of duties, tenure and promotion.[30] These assessments are vital for the creation of an honest, professional, and service-oriented police force.

The first step was designing and implementing a vetting model for the Federal Police[31] with this model contributing to the creation of a National Vetting Model that includes the following stages:

i) *Medical-toxicological evaluation*: the medical-toxicological stage previously consisted of a clinical interview and toxicological testing of urine samples. However, in order to obtain complete medical information, a comprehensive assessment program was designed and criteria established to guarantee the quality of diagnosis, transparency, objectivity, and homogeneity. Due to the adjustments made to this assessment stage, today we can establish whether a person being tested uses or has used drugs, along with the types of substances involved. We can also gather other relevant data on the health conditions of personnel, both of new officers and officers on active duty, in order to identify whether officers tested have or lack the skills and capacities necessary to perform their duties.

ii) *Psychological evaluation*: this is an essential test to discover whether the personality traits, work style, aptitudes and abilities of a candidate match the position profile. It further identifies a person's training needs in specific areas. The

---

30. Article 96 of the General Law of the National Public Security System establishes that police institutions should perform rigorous vetting of officers to establish whether they comply with personality, ethical and medical profiles on entry and during promotion and tenure procedures.

31. The Secretary of Public Security Vetting Center is one of the two Federal Vetting Centers that has already been certified by the National Certification and Accreditation Center.

current design of this stage enables us to receive additional information on a candidate, adding to what was obtained through psychometric testing, and cross-reference it with information from the other evaluation stages.

iii) *Polygraph evaluation*: this evaluation helps to establish whether new entry officers or officers on active duty have breached institutional guidelines. The interview process prior to use of the polygraph has been designed to detect clearly defined and standardized risk factors.

This evaluation stage is the responsibility of instructors recognized by the American Polygraph Association (APA) and a team of polygraphists certified in accordance with rigorous internationally accepted standards.

At the beginning of this Administration in December 2006 there were only 17 non-certified trained polygraphists who together conducted an average of 40 tests per day. At present there are 299 polygraphists with the capacity to conduct up to 500 evaluations a day. The first two generations (182 polygraphists) received training from institutions in Mexico, Israel and the United States of America –all certified by the APA– and the final three generations (117 polygraphists) were trained by the National Academy for Training and Investigation in Polygraph Analysis, part of the General Credibility Assessment Directorate (Vetting), which is also Certified by the APA. Due to this strengthening of institutional capacity, the number of tests performed have increased substantially, rising from an annual total of 24,943 in 2007 to 88,801 assessments in 2009, an increase of 256%.

iv) *Background investigation*: information previously obtained through socioeconomic investigation was of limited value since it was not cross-referenced against findings from other stages of the evaluation process. However, this stage of the evaluation now establishes whether there is consistency between the lifestyle of the person under evaluation and their professional, social, labor and economic track record. It also allows us to obtain information on criminal, personal and labor records, as well as follow up on officers dismissed from the force. The process is today divided into four stages: background information; documentary validation; socioeconomic investigation, which includes a home visit; along with analysis and interpretation of the data collected.

The following chart summarizes the vetting process and its differences to the old process:

Chart 5. Vetting: Improvement at Each Stage

Area Assessed	Previously	At Present
Medical-Toxicological Evaluation	Toxicology testing and clinical interview.	Comprehensive medical examination with laboratory and specialized tests.
Psychological Evaluation	Performed, but not differentially.	Applied differentially according to the testing program, position and duties to be performed.
Polygraph Evaluation	Performed without following internationally accepted parameters.	Performed in strict adherence to internationally accepted parameters.
Investigation into the socioeconomic background (Background investigation)	Documents were validated, but there was no follow-up. No home visits were made.	Documents are checked for authenticity, along with consistency of information submitted by the persons subject to evaluation. There is follow-up and home visits.

The aforementioned evaluations are conducted throughout an officer's professional development, specifically in the cases mentioned in the following chart:

Chart 6. Responsibilities and Objectives of the Vetting Process

Responsibility	Objective
Process incoming personnel	Identify competent and reliable individuals whose profile matches the requirements of the position and institutional values and principles.

Process personnel on active duty - Promotions - Changes to duties - Special commissions - Carrying of firearms - Performance evaluations	Security mechanism oriented towards making the service more professional, strengthening levels of security, reliability, aptitude, discipline and instruction to guarantee institutional operations and effectiveness. Likewise, determine preventive measures to safeguard the Secretary's security and personnel.
Support specific investigations	Define profiles and risk behavior in order to propose lines of investigation that assist law enforcement and strengthen public security.

The following chart provides a breakdown of figures according to type of assessment from 2006 through the first quarter of 2011.

Chart 7. Total Vetting Conducted by the Secretary of Public Security

(December 2006-March 2011)

Program	2006	2007	2008	2009	2010	March 2011
New Entry	156	18 140	18 616	55 239	27 255	8 588
Tenure, Group Formation and Promotion	306	327	7 366	5 088	15 310	3 656
Collective Official License	62	5 432	5 489	14 426	260	3 342
Special Assessments	0	254	390	416	152	6
External Support	0	790	42 700	13 632	2 451	294
Total	524	24 943	74 561	88 801	45 428	15 866

This significant increase in the Secretary of Public Security's abilities to apply vetting has required the equipping of clinical laboratories for the performance of toxicological analysis, as well as basic office check-ups, dentistry, optometry, radiology, electrocardiography, audiometry and general medicine.

4.1.2 Design of a National Vetting Model

The New Vetting Model created by the Secretary of Public Security supported the establishment of a National Model approved in November 2008 by the National Public Security Council. This permits the evaluation of all personnel in public security institutions at the three levels of government through the use of uniform criteria.

The National Vetting Model and the creation of certified State Vetting Centers were commitments of the National Agreement for Security, Justice and Lawfulness (*Acuerdo Nacional por la Seguridad, la Justicia y la Legalidad*, ANSJL) signed on August 21, 2008. Since then, the Federal Secretary of Public Security, the Center for Investigation and National Security and the National Certification and Accreditation Center (*Centro Nacional de Certificación y Acreditación*, CNCA) have promoted the creation and strengthening of state level Vetting Centers. At the request of states, advice has been provided on technological equipment and personnel selection and training.[32] To ensure that all Vetting Centers in the country operate according to the National Model, their assessment protocols have been reviewed and adapted.[33]

---

32. Advice has been given to the Federal District and the states of Chiapas, Guerrero, Yucatán, Mexico, Michoacán, Querétaro, Puebla, Baja California, Baja California Sur, Morelos, Tabasco, Chihuahua, Durango, Oaxaca, Tamaulipas, Veracruz, Hidalgo, Quintana Roo, Colima, Campeche, San Luis Potosí, Sinaloa, Jalisco, Coahuila, Guanajuato, Nuevo León and Sonora.

33. Through this follow-up and with the support of state authorities, there are currently:
- 13 State Vetting Centers with certified processes: Federal District (Secretary of Public Security), Sinaloa, Nuevo León-CISEC, Tamaulipas, State of Mexico, Aguascalientes, Coahuila, Veracruz-PGJ, Querétaro, Nuevo León-PGJ, Sonora, Morelos and Michoacán.
- 5 Centers undergoing certification: Chiapas, Chihuahua, Colima, Veracruz-CESP and Zacatecas.
- 13 Centers undergoing alignment to the National Model: Baja California Sur, Campeche, Federal District-CG, Durango, Guanajuato-PGJ, Guerrero, Jalisco, Oaxaca, Puebla-CESP-PGJ, Tabasco, Tlaxcala and Yucatán.
- 4 Centers being created: Hidalgo, Nayarit, San Luis Potosí and Veracruz-Secretary of Public Security.
- 1 state without a Vetting Center: Quintana Roo.

Thanks to the design and implementation of the National Vetting Model, the fundamentals were provided for purging the country's police forces and supporting the entry and tenure of officers with the right profile for the performance of public security duties.[34]

4.2 Professional Development Master Program

The second component of the Police Comprehensive Development System is the Professional Development Master Program, which establishes the set of educational programs for public servants in the police forces belonging to the three levels of government.[35] The main objective of this Program is to standardize basic training and continuing education for Federal Police officers and other police forces in Mexico, guaranteeing that officers have the basic knowledge to perform their duties and the chance to further themselves academically while growing professionally in their police career. The Program syllabi have been designed for the purpose of developing the necessary knowledge, skills and aptitudes to perform public security duties.

Syllabi Objectives and Design

The Professional Development Master Program was designed with a focus on the duties, responsibilities and profiles of police officers in their three main functions: Investigation, Prevention and Response, and the thirteen hierarchical levels. Using this as a starting point, training needs were defined and the courses for each police rank designed.

For the purposes of implementation, the Professional Development Master Program defined specific courses for basic training, refresher courses, and specialization for promotion.

---

34. One example of support provided to police forces by the Secretary of Public Security in other government sectors is that during the period from November 27, 2008 to the first quarter of 2011, 2,406 officers from a total of 2,618 in the Specialized Units for Combating Kidnapping were vetted, an advance of 91.9%.

35. The strategy and guidelines for implementing Police Development System and the content of the Professional Development Master Program were approved at the National Conference of Public Security Secretaries held on March 2, 2009 and ratified at the Twenty-Seventh Session of the National Public Security Council held on November 26, 2009.

The Program establishes that for entry at the Police officer level a candidate is required to take the six-month Basic Training Course. It also defines the refresher courses officers will require in order to advance through the ranks of Police Officer 3, Police Officer 2, Police Officer 1, Deputy Officer, Officer and Deputy Inspector.

In the case of candidates entering the police force directly with the rank of Deputy Officer with higher education, the Program states that they must take the corresponding Basic Training course lasting six months, which includes Basic Officer Training courses for Police Officers, and courses needed to rise through the ranks of Police Officer 3, Police Officer 2 and Police Officer 1.

To rise to the rank of Inspector, Chief Inspector or General Inspector, candidates must complete the Specialization courses in order to be promoted. These have two components: the first, intermediate training, seeks to raise the technical capacities of officers in the areas of Investigation, Prevention and Response. The second is specific training to prepare experts in the different Federal Police divisions. Each division will have the required number of specialties based on the areas comprising it.

Finally, the Professional Development Master Program incorporates Senior Management courses for the highest rank (Commissioner level). This Program is intended to develop knowledge, capacities and skills for planning, managing and evaluating human resources and materials, essential elements for the operation and management of a police force.

National and International collaboration in designing the Professional Development Master Program

The Professional Development Master Program was designed by the Federal Police in collaboration with representatives from various state public security secretaries. Additional contributions were made by experts from public-security forces in Canada, Chile, Colombia, Spain and the United States of America. This Program, applicable throughout Mexico's police forces, provides the tools to develop attributes and skills required by officers when performing their duties. As part of the effort to use the model for other levels of government, the curricular structure of the Professional Development Master Program represents 80% of the academic and technical content of the career, while the remaining 20% is comprised of professional development requirements agreed with states. The purpose is to provide specific police training related to the most common regional problems requiring attention.

The following actions have been taken to implement the Professional Development Master Program:

i) *Federal Police Recruitment Program*: in keeping with the new profiles required by the New Public Security Model, an institutional effort was made to incorporate a new generation of professionals into the Federal Police. In 2009 the Federal Police Recruitment Program was launched with the Scientific and Intelligence Investigator Profile, bringing thousands of university students from across the country into the institution's ranks.

Within the framework of this Program, the Secretary of Public Security established collaborative agreements with some of the most prestigious universities in Mexico with the goal of recruiting young graduates. In addition, joint efforts were made so that professors from these universities could participate in training Federal Police officers.[36] Thanks to the cooperation of these educational institutions and the academic community, more than 4,400 youngsters with Bachelor's degrees and, in some cases graduate degrees, have joined the ranks of the Federal Police. The following chart summarizes the results of the Federal Police recruiting and entry program:

Chart 8: Recruitment and Selection of Federal Police Officers with a Scientific Investigation Profile

Within the framework of the 2009 Recruiting Program

Total Vetting Applied	Number of Candidates Meeting the Profile	Number of Candidates Starting Courses	Number of Graduates
23 078	7 515	5 198	4 464

36. To that end agreements were signed with the National Association of Universities and Higher Education Institutions (ANUIES - acronym in Spanish) and various universities such as the Universidad Anáhuac, the Instituto Tecnológico y de Estudios Superiores de Monterrey (ITESM), Universidad Iberoamericana (UIA), Universidad La Salle, Universidad Tecnológica de Mexico (Unitec), Instituto Politécnico Nacional (IPN), Universidad Autónoma Metropolitana (UAM), El Colegio de Mexico (Colmex), Universidad del Valle de Mexico (UVM), Instituto Tecnológico Autónomo de Mexico (ITAM) and Secretary of Public Education (SEP) Technical Colleges.
37. It is very important to point out that of the total number of officers recruited 40% are women.

More than 8,000 university graduates are currently using their abilities and professional training to contribute to the tasks of investigation, analysis and intelligence with the Federal Police.

As a complement to this first stage of collaboration with academic institutions, the Secretary of Public Security signed another agreement in February 2011 with prestigious scientific research institutes and higher education institutions to perform joint actions in, among other areas, multi-disciplinary research and studies on topics related to public security.[38]

As part of the institutional transformation of the Secretary of Public Security, major changes to the entry profiles for all Federal Police ranks have been encouraged, including higher ranks. Proof of this is the incorporation of professionals with graduate degrees from national and foreign universities into Federal Police management positions.

ii) *Basic Training for Scientific and Intelligence Investigation Officers*: this course is given to professionals as part of the Federal Police Scientific and Intelligence Investigator entry process. Successful completion of the course ensures they have the theoretical and practical knowledge required to perform

38. The signatory institutions are: Academia Mexicana de Ciencias, Centro de Investigación y Docencia Económicas, El Colegio de Mexico, Consejo Mexicano de Ciencias Sociales, Escuela Libre de Derecho, Facultad Latinoamericana de Ciencias Sociales (Mexico City campus), Instituto de Investigaciones Dr. José María Luís Mora, Instituto Universitario de Investigación Ortega y Gasset Mexico, Instituto Mexicano del Petróleo, Instituto Nacional de Administración Pública, Instituto Nacional de Medicina Genómica, Instituto Politécnico Nacional, Instituto Tecnológico Autónomo de Mexico, Instituto Tecnológico y de Estudios Superiores de Monterrey, Universidad Anáhuac, Universidad Autónoma Metropolitana, Universidad del Valle de Mexico, Universidad Iberoamericana, Universidad La Salle, Universidad Nacional Autónoma de Mexico, Universidad Tecnológica de Mexico, Secretary of Public Education Technical Colleges and the Asociación Nacional de Universidades e Instituciones de Educación Superior (National Association of Further Education Universities and Institutions) .

39. The course lasts for a period of 3 months, includes a total of 598 hours training and requires full-time attendance. Subsequently, 440 hours (2 months) of specialized knowledge in specific areas such as Investigation, Intelligence and Anti-drugs are programmed. The course concludes with a month of tutorials.

police duties.[39] The course subjects are organized into the following modules: Police Doctrine and Ethics, Police Techniques and Tactics, Principles of Police Analysis and Investigation, and Complementary Subjects (such as Criminal and Procedural Law). In order to achieve high level training, the 2009 mass recruitment program involved instructors from the Secretary of Public Security and the Federal Police, as well as experts from prestigious international institutions.[40]

iii) *Continuous Training*: in order to continually develop the attributes, capacities, and skills of police force officers, a continuing education process was implemented with refresher, specialty, promotion and senior management courses.[41]

Preparing Federal Police operational forces includes providing refresher courses in long-barreled weapons marksmanship, investigation methodology and techniques, covert operations, immediate response to bomb threats, and personal defense.

Furthermore, since fighting such crimes as drug trafficking, money laundering, kidnapping and extortion requires specific knowledge and skills, Federal Police officers receive continuous and specialized training on topics such as the legal panorama of organized crime, financial investigation techniques, prevention and

---

40. During the 2009 recruitment program, the Policía Nacional de Colombia, Guardia Civil Española, Netherlands Police Agency, Czech Republic National Drug Squad, Royal Canadian Mounted Police, and various police institutions from the USA such as the U.S. Immigration and Customs Enforcement, U.S. Marshals, the Bureau of Alcohol, Tobacco, Firearms and Explosives (ATF), the Drug Enforcement Administration (DEA) and the Federal Bureau of Investigation (FBI) participated in training processes.

41. It is important to emphasize that the Federal Secretary of Public Security has supported the training of personnel from state and municipal police institutions. For example, as of the first quarter of 2011, 1,615 instructors on different subjects had been accredited, in addition to the training of 6,829 officers on topics such as Information Analysis and Plataforma Mexico Tools, among others. In addition, due to commitments established at the Fourth National Conference of Public Security Secretaries held in November 2010 at the Superior Academy of San Luis Potosí, the Secretary of Public Security trained 177 State Police Investigation Unit officers from the states of Colima, Guanajuato, the State of Mexico, Oaxaca and Veracruz.

detection of operations with resources of illicit origin, information analysis and treatment, advanced interview and non-verbal communication techniques, and undercover agent training.[42]

The Operational Management course, designed for deputy officers, officers and deputy inspectors, includes such topics as arms, drug and human trafficking, and money laundering. The aim of this course is to train officers to assume leadership positions and accept greater responsibility within the force.

The course in Senior Management, designed for the highest rank, is for developing knowledge, capacities and skills for the planning, administration and evaluation of human and material resources. Relevant topics taught as part of the course include organized crime in Mexico, institutional development, police techniques and tactics, police management and operations, and strategic communications.[43]

Federal Police officers also receive training in human rights since this topic is a fundamental component of institutional policy. Of special note is the signing of two agreements with the International Red Cross to provide training for police officers in human rights and humanitarian principles. The first was signed on June 12, 2008 and the second on February 14, 2011.

Personnel have also been trained in the Istanbul Protocol regarding Torture Prevention and Diagnosis,

---

42. In addition, and in order to strengthen the professional development of Federal Police officers, the Secretary of Public Security has established training agreements with several countries and international organizations. For example, the Inter-American Police Training Program of the OAS, the Latin American and Caribbean Intelligence Community/ Latin American Commanders, Directors and Chiefs of Police of Latin America and the Caribbean (CLACIP), and the American Police Community (Ameripol).

43. 42 high ranking officers from Federal Police and Federal Police State Center divisions participated in the first course. Other participating experts were from well-known police institutions such as the Policía Nacional de Colombia, the FBI, and the Royal Canadian Mounted Police, who gave specialized courses such as Police Intelligence, Criminal Investigation, Strategic Planning, Crisis Management and Negotiations, and Leadership. These courses allow high ranking Federal Police officers to strengthen and acquire knowledge and skills related to best practices.

which is applicable to prison centers and the performance of police operations and detentions. Finally, in order to safeguard the human rights of migrants, the Secretary of Public Security implemented a teaching program on interview techniques and the applicable legal framework.[44]

iv) *Academic Leveling*: A number of steps have been taken to raise the academic profile of Federal Police officers, including the unveiling of a National Accreditation Study Day in conjunction with the National Institute for Adult Education (*Instituto Nacional para la Educación de Adultos*, INEA) so that police officers could accredit their primary and secondary studies. Several additional actions have been taken so that officers can accredit their high-school education[45] and their Professional Technical High-School studies.[46]

v) *Promotion Process*: as an important step in the introduction of the Professional Police Career Service, in 2008 the first promotions process since the creation of the Federal Preventive Police in 1999 was conducted. Some 1,665

---

44. Personnel trained in the framework of this teaching program include more than 200 Federal Police officers stationed at the country's principal airports.

45. Through Agreement 286, a provision issued by the Secretary of Public Education (*Secretaría de Educación Pública*, SEP), it is now possible to accredit educational levels such as high-school diplomas through an examination determining whether the knowledge and abilities of the police under evaluation are equivalent to those acquired by persons studying formally. This method of assessment is an alternative for those who were unable to study or finish high school but have acquired sufficient knowledge, whether self-taught or through work experience. More than 6,000 police officers have taken these tests with 90% obtaining their certificate of studies, which is an unprecedented number of successful results. In addition, in order to contribute to the professional development of Federal Police officers and acknowledge the career path and the experience of officers forming part of this institution with a diploma and professional identification, in conjunction with the SEP and the National Center of Evaluation for Higher Education (Ceneval – acronym in Spanish) and on the basis of the aforementioned agreement, on-duty personnel of the Federal Police were given a general knowledge examination serving to accredit the level of Superior University Technician or Professional Technician in Public Security. As of the first quarter of 2011, 4,005 police officers had received diplomas and professional identification as Superior University Technicians.

46. Through the collaboration of the National College of Technical Professional Education (Conalep), a day was established to promote obtaining this level of studies for Federal Police officers.

officers received promotions after having successfully completed the necessary evaluations and requirements corresponding to the rank applied for. This effectively represented public recognition for the efforts and dedication of police officers while also providing them with better wages in recognition of an outstanding career trajectory. In 2011, 4,038 federal police were promoted.

vi) *Superior Academy of Public Security*: the Superior Academy of Public Security was developed to provide support for the Professional Development Master Program. This Academy was restored in 2007 and has become a major source of support in the training of new officers and officers on active duty. To meet its responsibilities the Academy underwent major remodeling and its facilities were adapted to the training needs of the Professional Development Master Program. This made it possible to train 13,802 officers from the first quarter of 2007 through the first quarter of 2011, both in basic training courses and continuing education and international courses.[47]

4.3 Disciplinary Regime

The third component of the Police Comprehensive Development System is the disciplinary regime designed to evaluate cases of possible deviation from duty in police actions due to non-compliance with the Institution's master principles or violations of the regulatory framework –with the levying of appropriate sanctions. Discipline is the foundation of the organization and the performance of any police force so a regime was designed to establish the rules and incentives required to motivate Federal Police officers to perform their duties with honor and professionalism.

---

47. This academy currently has eighteen classrooms and six computer rooms, a large auditorium with space for 176 people, two auditoriums, two driving simulators, three open firing ranges and one closed electronic simulator for firing at 50 meters, a documentation center, heliport, obstacle course, driver education (perimetral, urban and curves), a medical unit, crime laboratories, rooms for housing 1,000 students and 42 instructors, a mess hall, auditorium, gym, covered pool and courts for different sports activities.

The Federal Police Development Council was created in order for the disciplinary regime to be effective and is responsible for regulating, hearing and resolving all disputes related to disciplinary regime procedures, the Professional Career Service and professional development.[48] This Council has permanent representatives from all areas of the Federal Police: a Chairperson (who is the General Commissioner), a General Secretary, a representative from the Internal Control Office (*Órgano Interno de Control*, OIC), a representative from the Legal Unit of the Secretary of Public Security, a Council member from each operational area, and a Council member from the legal department of the Federal Police. Clearly defined sanctions were also established, ranging from warnings to removal from a position. In the latter case both the General Law of the National Public Security System and Federal Police Law prohibit the rehiring of or compensation for sanctioned individuals, irrespective of the proceedings or means of defense.

Creation of the aforementioned agencies, along with the implementation of new Federal Police disciplinary regime legal provisions, have made it possible to reward police officers through providing recognition and incentives for outstanding actions. In addition, a firm sanctions policy was introduced for those who break the rules and violate the institution's principles. Under this regime and as part of a Federal Council on Police Development resolution, during the first quarter of 2011, 3,200 officers were dismissed for non-compliance with requirements established by the different provisions of the General Law of the National Public Security System, as well as for non-compliance with the duties described in Federal Police Law. At that time, disciplinary measures were instituted against another 1,063 officers for their failure to comply with tenure requirements, specifically for not having passed the corresponding vetting.

A systematic process has been established to purge the Federal Police of officers who violate the provisions of legal duties they should observe. In cases when the probable participation of an officer in the commission of illegal acts is detected, the corresponding report is brought before the competent authorities and filed.

Federal Police Development Council

Meritocracy for Promotions and Recognition

Sanctions for Failure to Perform Police Duties

Systematic Process for Purging the Federal Police

---

48. Federal Police Manual of the Federal Council on Police Development was published in the Official Gazette of the Federation.

This forms part of the actions necessary to review and purge the Federal Police, a key element in consolidating the New Public Security Model. The Police Development System Disciplinary Regime, the Internal Affairs Unit, and the Federal Council on Police Development are the instruments used to ensure the tenure of only those officers whose actions are bound by law and the institutional principles of the Federal Police.

4.4 Complementary Social Security System

Improvements in
Social Security
Conditions
for Police

For a long time insufficient attention was paid to the conditions by which police officers provided their services and no recognition was paid to the fact that officer duties involved risks and demands unlike any other job. Consequently, in order to consolidate the career of police officer and ensure that good officers remain, all officers and their families must enjoy a better standard of living. Accordingly, the purpose of the Complementary Social Security System is to improve health, social and labor services to take better care of the country's police officers.

Scope of the Complementary Social Security System:

- Improve the quality of personal, family and social life.
- Develop a sense of belonging to the Police Force.
- Have adequate and timely risk protection against sickness, disability, aging or death.

Benefits should include the following areas:

- Medical: hospitalization and sickness care.
- Economic: short and medium-term loans, housing funds, compensation coverage for professional risks, life insurance, and retirement on the basis of age, years of service, or disability.
- Social and cultural: sports facilities and socio-cultural events.

***

The Police Comprehensive Development System establishes the foundations for strengthening the Federal Police as well as a nationwide model that encourages the development of police forces through the creation of the conditions, processes and incentives necessary to guarantee the reliability, professionalization and development of Mexico's police officers.

Conclusions

THE NEW PUBLIC SECURITY MODEL FOR MEXICO

RESTRUCTURING THE FEDERAL POLICE

5. Restructuring the Federal Police

Although the foundations needed for human and technological resources were in place, a restructuring of the Federal Police was essential to improve its logistical and operational capacities. An explanation of how the police force was reorganized so that both the new legal features and investment in human resources and technology were translated into efficient strategies and actions to confront organized crime, along with other forms of criminality, will be given over the course of the following pages.

First, the Federal Police was restructured into divisions entrusted with specific and complementary tasks so the police force as a whole could operate in line with each stage of the intelligence cycle. Sections 1 and 2 of this Chapter describe this restructuring.

Second, it was vital to have a command center for operations that could develop capacities in different areas while at the same time making it possible to ensure closer coordination between police forces and state and municipal authorities. The Federal Police Command Center was created with this goal in mind. Additionally, it was necessary to create agencies throughout Mexico entrusted with replicating the New Public Security Model based on the intelligence cycle so Federal Police State Centers were created to accomplish this. These institutions allow the Federal Police to maintain its presence and operate in states and were designed to comply with each stage of the aforementioned intelligence cycle. These issues will be covered in Section 3.

To provide support for the restructuring of the Federal Police, unprecedented efforts were made to increase Police Strength in line with new profiles and required standards. This led to a tripling of the number of officers in a period of just three years. In addition, police force infrastructure and equipment were modernized; these issues will be covered in Section 4.

Police Strength, Infrastructure and Equipment

Finally, actions and programs have been introduced to guarantee that Federal Police adopt standardized procedures in strict compliance with the law and with respect for human rights. In addition, mechanisms have been introduced to encourage citizen participation in crime prevention and the reporting of crimes based on a culture of lawfulness. These issues will be covered in the final three sections.

5.1 New Operational Capacities of the Federal Police

In order to operate in accordance with the different stages of the intelligence basic cycle the Federal Police was restructured into six divisions. These divisions oversee the planning, gathering, analysis and use of information generated using Plataforma Mexico technological tools. Restructuring has allowed the Federal Police to perform different tasks such as operations designed to maintain public order, dismantle organized crime organizations, and fight crime through the use of police intelligence. The six Federal Police Divisions are:

i) *Investigative Division*: this Division is responsible for gathering information in the field using human sources and technical services. It also creates tactical databases and criminal files. Through analytical work the Division produces input for the areas responsible for intelligence generation.

ii) *Intelligence Division*: this Division is responsible for analyzing information that helps generate police intelligence in order to identify *modus operandi*, persons, groups and organizations allegedly linked to crimes falling under Federal Police jurisdiction. In addition, the Intelligence Division is responsible for coordinating technical support for the other divisions.

iii) *Scientific Division*: this Division operates the forensic and criminalistic laboratories, and coordinates their work with intelligence activities in order to use science and technology efficiently when searching for, obtaining and preserving evidence essential to preventing and fighting crime. The Division also has a technological innovation area which, through links with national and international academic institutions, generates applied technology options for Federal Police operations. It is also responsible for overseeing and monitoring the Internet to prevent crimes being committed.

iv) *Antidrug Division*: this Division is responsible for combating the production, possession, trafficking and other illegal activities related to narcotics and psychotropic drugs. It also fights crimes associated with transactions involving illicit funds.

v) *Federal Forces Division*: this Division participates in operations implemented or coordinated by the Federal Police and in high-impact operations, using highly trained and specialized response personnel. In addition its officers assist the general public in the event of emergencies or disasters.

vi) *Regional Security Division*: through Federal Police State Centers, this division is responsible for replicating the intelligence basic cycle in each state thereby enabling efficient operation of the Federal Police throughout the country. The Division also is responsible for guaranteeing public security along federal communication routes, at ports and at airports.

The redesign of the Federal Police has increased institutional capacities for the prevention and combating of federal crimes. The following section explains how the police force operates according to the new model of intelligence generation and scientific crime investigation.

Figure 3. Structure of the Federal Police

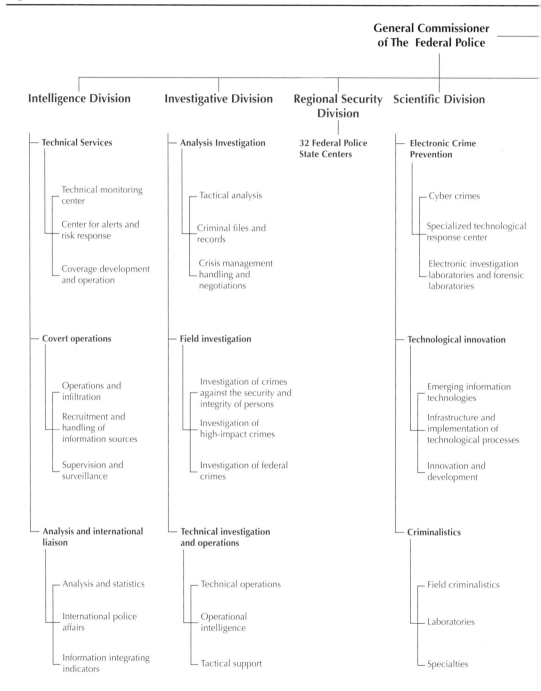

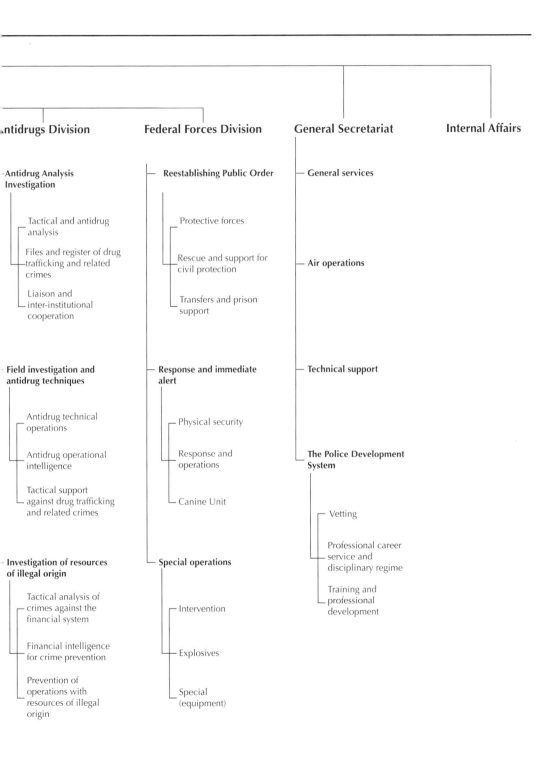

ntidrugs Division

— **Antidrug Analysis Investigation**

  ⌐ Tactical and antidrug analysis

  ⌐ Files and register of drug trafficking and related crimes

  ⌐ Liaison and inter-institutional cooperation

— **Field investigation and antidrug techniques**

  ⌐ Antidrug technical operations

  ⌐ Antidrug operational intelligence

  ⌐ Tactical support against drug trafficking and related crimes

— **Investigation of resources of illegal origin**

  ⌐ Tactical analysis of crimes against the financial system

  ⌐ Financial intelligence for crime prevention

  ⌐ Prevention of operations with resources of illegal origin

Federal Forces Division

— **Reestablishing Public Order**

  ⌐ Protective forces

  ⌐ Rescue and support for civil protection

  ⌐ Transfers and prison support

— **Response and immediate alert**

  ⌐ Physical security

  ⌐ Response and operations

  ⌐ Canine Unit

— **Special operations**

  ⌐ Intervention

  ⌐ Explosives

  ⌐ Special (equipment)

General Secretariat

— **General services**

— **Air operations**

— **Technical support**

— **The Police Development System**

  ⌐ Vetting

  ⌐ Professional career service and disciplinary regime

  ⌐ Training and professional development

Internal Affairs

5.2 Operation of the Federal Police Intelligence Basic Cycle

In general terms, the intelligence cycle is a continuous process of planning, gathering and analyzing information, as well as the development of products that will help police forces adopt strategies to fight crime. In order to perform the tasks involved in the intelligence cycle, the Federal Police has undergone an in-depth process of transformation that provides it with an organizational structure and methodology suitable to the efficient performance of its duties. As explained below, Federal Police divisions interact and participate in the different stages of the intelligence cycle to achieve specialization in their specific areas of duty and to prevent corruption and possible information leaks. To that end, information is segmented according to the duties and responsibilities of each area.

5.2.1 Planning and Information Gathering

1st stage:
Planning

2nd stage:
Planning

During the first stage of the cycle, planning, the design strategies of different divisions are prioritized and defined in order to generate actions aimed at crime prevention and to investigate and resolve crimes that have already been committed. Planning then allows the scope and goals of the second stage of the cycle to be fixed by gathering substantive crime information through the scientific analysis of circumstantial evidence related to the facts. Information gathering is performed through such activities as:

i) *Information gathering and the establishing of a criminal database*: the Federal Police has operational structures and trained units that work on establishing tactical databanks and criminal files. The information fed into these databases comes from a variety of sources:

Sources for Criminal Databases
- Criminal data gathered in public places.
- Complaints received in the terms of applicable provisions.
- Information exchanged with authorities from the three levels of government and with foreign police forces.
- Standardized police reports.
- Undercover and infiltration operations for the purpose of gathering information on the structure of organized crime, modus operandi and spheres of action.
- Communications intervention through the prior issuing of court orders.
- Information requested from telecommunications services companies through a previously issued court order.

The data gathered is loaded into Unified Criminal Information System databases so they can be searched, analyzed and used during the following stages of the intelligence cycle.

ii) *Scientific Crime Investigation*: the Scientific Division collects evidence for the purpose of identifying subjects, scenarios, motives, procedures, equipment, and any officers involved in the committing of a crime.

This Division –created to comply with the new powers conferred on Federal Police for the scientific investigation of crime– is able to secure a crime scene, the integrity of evidence, fingerprints or traces, the instruments, objects or results of crime, complying at all times with the "custody chain of evidence." This refers to evidence follow-up, from locating and preserving evidence to its evaluation by judges to prevent its alteration, substitution, deterioration, contamination or destruction. Data and information gathered through this process serve as inputs for intelligence generation as they provide elements for the scientific investigation of crimes and are uploaded onto Plataforma Mexico databases. By obtaining fingerprints, biometric data, photographs and videos, among other elements, the Scientific Division can constantly update criminal and public security personnel databases on Plataforma Mexico. This task is fundamental to the analysis of information performed by other areas of the Federal Police. With this guidance, the Federal Police is developing capacities for the operation of forensic and crime laboratories (such as toxicological and genetic laboratories) that process all evidence at their disposal using the highest levels of technical specificity. Through the scientific analysis of evidence it is possible to establish the foundations for moving beyond the old paradigm that in order for criminals to be charged they must be caught *in flagrante* since it is now possible to provide useful evidence in court. This enables the Public Prosecutor's Office to conduct more sound and objective investigations and helps generate major legal certainty for the public during law enforcement actions and the administration of justice.

iii) *Gathering Evidence Digitally*: the development of technological and computer systems led to the emergence of criminal behavior directed against the security of persons and their property in the form of fraud, threats, child pornography and the corruption of minors. Given the increase in this new form of criminality, a specialized area has been created to prevent and fight this type of crime.

To fight so-called "cyber-crime" this area, which belongs to the Scientific Division, has two main functions: first it has a system for monitoring Internet sites and identifying acts that constitute a crime, and second, it is geared towards obtaining digital evidence of the illegal acts committed. It operates electronics, computer and telecommunications laboratories to analyze systems and equipment (such as cell phones, computers, PDAs, and USBs) that may have been used improperly. This area also proposes solutions for cases related to hacking and phishing and for the neutralization of electronic sites that may be used to harm the public. Information gathered as part of these analyses is incorporated and compared with information already held in Plataforma Mexico databases.

5.2.2 Information Analysis

For this third stage of the intelligence cycle the Federal Police analyzes information gathered and included in databases for the purpose of identifying persons involved in criminal actions or organized crime.

Through the Investigative, Intelligence and Antidrug Divisions, Unified Criminal Information System (SUIC) databases are used to conduct investigations based on the objective evaluation of facts and projections –not on the intuition or preconceived ideas of investigators. In other words, intelligence is generated for the purpose of understanding and analyzing trends and patterns in criminal activity, which among other things contributes to the clarification of facts, the identification of criminal modus operandi, and the identification and location of participants in illegal acts for the purposes of dismantling criminal structures.

The final product of the intelligence process is the result of analytical treatment of data gathered from a variety of sources (communications intervention, covert and infiltration operations, Standardized Police Reports, etc.) This process is translated into intelligence inputs so the Federal Police can perform its duties. Examples of the aforementioned inputs are:

Intelligence Input

i) Linked networks: cross-referenced information that confirms or denies relationships or associations between persons or organizations, as well as between domiciles, vehicles, weapons, communications equipment, and certain situational factors that may help strengthen lines of investigation.

ii) Analytical networks: graphic information that shows the correlation of events between two or more cases for the purpose of identifying a "similarity in modus operandi," which in turn permits a comprehensive explanation of different criminal facts.

iii) Crime maps: geo-referencing of an event or the behavior of an individual or organization under investigation.

Intelligence generation inputs such as the above respond to the goals established at the first stage and when this information is consolidated and correlated it helps determine the behavior of criminals, in particular criminals and organized crime organizations under investigation. The role of police is therefore not limited to arresting criminals caught in flagrante since the use of substantive information allows them to attack criminal structures and their logistics: money, communications, supplies and operations.

5.2.3 Exploitation of Police Intelligence

The generation of police intelligence now makes it possible to motivate and determine the types of action needed for fighting crime; including searches, the arrest of persons or groups, and the performance of operations in specific regions of the country. The Federal Forces Division has been strengthened and professionalized to work on these activities.

This Division uses applications from Plataforma Mexico, such as the Operational Management System, offering precise information on the equipment and police officers available for planning and performing an operation in specific circumstances.

Similarly, the Federal Forces Division performs operations related to disturbances or situations affecting public order; it intervenes in crisis situations (such as hostage-taking and prison riots) and even participates in civil protection programs such as natural disasters. This Division is also involved in joint operations to inspect and oversee areas with high crime rates and participates at checkpoints established in strategic areas throughout the country.

In order to perform its duties, this Division adopts the necessary measures to provide protection and immediate assistance to the victims of and witnesses to crimes who, in many cases, provide information that greatly assists the intelligence cycle. Due to the diversity of the operations it can perform, the Federal Forces Division has several highly trained units that contribute to the performance of its duties:

i)   *Unit for Reestablishing Public Order* (*Unidad para el Reestablecimiento del Orden Público*, UROP): the main function of this unit is to support operations involving federal crimes and provide external surveillance and security for key government institutions.

ii) *Unit for the Transfer of Inmates and Protection of Federal Social Reintegration Centers (Unidad para el Traslado de Reos y Resguardo de Centros Federales de Readaptación Social)*: this unit is responsible for securing these facilities and also performs operations for the seizure of weapons, drugs and illicit money, in addition to assisting in riot control and the transfer of inmates.

iii) *Rescue and Public Assistance Unit (Unidad de Rescate y Auxilio Social*, URAS)*: this Unit assists the public in the event of natural disasters.

iv) *Special Operations Unit (Grupo Especial de Operaciones* GEO)*: this Unit has been given greater technological and human resources to perform high-impact operations. Officers in this unit are highly trained in such areas as tactical deployment, crisis situation intervention and resolution, the arrest of extremely dangerous criminals, and subduing prison riots.

The Federal Forces Division has the most modern methods at its disposal to face any type of contingency associated with Federal Police duties. One example would be a bomb squad equipped with cutting-edge technology including robots and disruptive cannons to locate, neutralize and deactivate explosive devices. The division has trained snipers, personnel specialized in skyjacking intervention operations, and canine teams for coordinating the detection of narcotics, weapons, explosive devices and banknotes, as well as to aid in the search and recovery of bodies.

To strengthen its new capacities for guaranteeing public security, the Federal Police has acquired seven Black Hawk S-70 helicopters featuring cutting-edge technology. These have also been specially equipped for the performance of Federal Police operations and for transferring specialized units anywhere in Mexico where their skills may be required. Three additional helicopters were acquired as part of the Mérida Initiative.

5.3 Projection of the New Public Security Model Nationwide

In order to respond effectively to the security needs of each state or region of the country, operational restructuring of the Federal Police has included the design of a new coordination plan through the creation of the Regional Security Division. Through the Federal Police Command Center, this Division performs tasks designed to comply with the different stages of the intelligence cycle at the 32 Federal Police State Centers. The objective is for the New Public Security Model to be replicated in each state since it represents an attempt to establish a proximity liaison with the citizenry. Police actions achieve better results when there is a closer relationship with the public since this permits more timely intervention in any criminal incident or activity. Next, a description is given of how Federal Police State Centers work.

Federal Police State Centers were created in 2008 and have areas specializing in the gathering, processing, classification and analysis of information, as well as special response units that help prevent and fight crime across the country. Due to their power to make immediate decisions and coordinate actions and operations more effectively in each state, these Federal Police State Centers serve as command units that enjoy full autonomy and make a genuine decentralization of the Federal Police possible.[49]

---

49. "Agreement 05/2008 of the Secretary of Public Security, which establishes the Federal Police State Centers of the Federal Police" was issued considering that: "in order to coordinate the efforts of the different areas deployed in national territory, and to avoid dispersion of resources and tasks in the struggle to strengthen public security, it is necessary to name, in each state, a public servant who will coordinate the different areas of the Federal Police so that the latter may work under a single command that directs, supervises and controls these areas, thereby establishing, within a defined jurisdiction, a standardized, uniform and organized structure that guarantees a permanent means of communication and feedback regarding its activities within the different areas of the Federal Police, of this agency of the Federal Executive, and of the states and municipalities to which support is provided."

Each Federal Police State Center has:
- A liaison with the Command and Intelligence Center. - Investigative Units.[50] - Preventive Security responsible for preventing and dealing with federal crimes throughout the country. - Federal Forces. - Prevention Liaisons responsible for promoting and developing a comprehensive public policy across the country concerning the prevention of crime and respect for human rights.

Figure 4. Structure of Federal Police State Centers

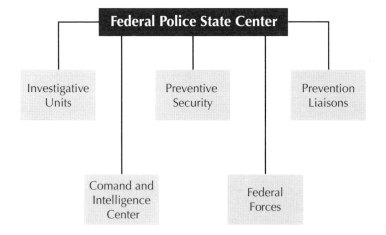

---

50. As of the first quarter of 2011, the Secretary of Public Security had trained 973 officers from these units in diverse areas such as Analysis and Criminal Intelligence, Criminal Investigation, and Evidence Preservation, among others.

5.4 Police Strength, Infrastructure, and Equipment

5.4.1 Police Strength

To strengthen the effectiveness of territorial deployments across Mexico and to guarantee compliance with the new duties assigned to Federal Police, the force has increased its number of active officers. As the following chart shows, the number of active officers has practically tripled over a period of three years:

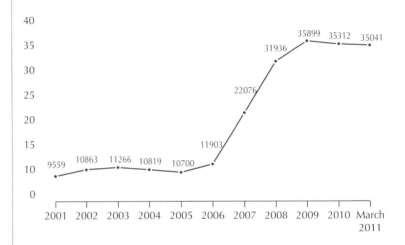

5.4.2 Infrastructure

New Federal Police stations have the technological equipment necessary to connect with Plataforma Mexico and maintain continuous communications with all other Federal Police stations through the exchange of voice recordings, data and video, as well as to other police forces at the three levels of government entrusted with public security and law enforcement. Equipped with facilities for training and preparation activities, as well as dormitories for housing Federal Police officers, these stations help ensure timely and effective operational response and police deployment. To promote increased contact with the public, the stations have also been equipped with areas for receiving complaints and assisting crime victims.

15 new police stations resembling the Command Center operating in Mexico City are currently under construction and should become operational during the course of 2011. In addition to these 15 new stations, a Command Center was built in Ciudad Juárez, Chihuahua, with special operational characteristics.[51] In a parallel fashion, a program to remodel existing local police stations is underway to make them more functional. A pilot program to improve the infrastructure of Federal Police control posts at entry and exit points to the country's main highways is also underway.

Due to the obsolescence of infrastructure for police canine team certification, there is currently a project to build a Canine Academy in Tepic, Nayarit. Existing buildings will be remodeled to provide the appropriate infrastructure and capacities to train canine teams in accordance with the operational needs of Federal and State Police.

Canine/Trainer Teams

In turn, new Intelligence and Scientific Police buildings contribute to criminal and personnel database uploading and the updating of Plataforma Mexico. These buildings also have areas for criminal investigation work equipped with forensic chemistry, forensic biology and narcotics laboratories; toxicological, photography, digital-imaging and fingerprint laboratories, as well as areas for indentifying firearms and DNA.

Intelligence and Scientific Police Buildings

5.4.3 Equipment

The deterioration of police forces is evidenced by aging and antiquated equipment and this made it necessary for the Federal Police to increase operational capacities through the acquisition of cutting-edge equipment and technology in order to respond to current public security needs. The following table provides a brief list, by way of example, of the efforts made to rectify this situation:

---

51. These are located in the cities of Querétaro, Querétaro; Uruapan, Michoacán; Hermosillo, Sonora; Tlalnepantla, State of Mexico; Cuernavaca, Morelos; Matamoros, Tamaulipas; Chihuahua, Chihuahua; Tijuana, Baja California; Veracruz, Veracruz; Tapachula, Chiapas; Matehuala, San Luis Potosí; Aguascalientes, Aguascalientes; Tepatitlán, Jalisco; Culiacán, Sinaloa; and Mazatlán, Sinaloa.

Chart 9. Federal Police Equipment

Tactical uniforms	Uniforms include means of identification, protection, durability, flexibility and adaptability to different climates. Federal Police officers also have tactical-type bulletproof vests with high levels of protection.
Communications equipment	In order for Federal Police officers to remain in constant contact with Plataforma Mexico, wireless access applications have been developed for the exchange of information and access to police force databases. These technologies make it possible, for example, to check the status of warrants and court orders and search for information on stolen vehicles and blacklisted persons. To monitor and identify the precise location of ground patrol units the Federal Police now has GPS and PDA equipment.
Vehicular and aircraft equipment	In 2010, 1,163 new radio-patrol cars had already been incorporated, in addition to armored vehicles, ambulances and mobile kitchens. The air fleet has gradually been replaced with aircraft using advanced air navigation equipment to guarantee competitive service in terms of maintenance and fuel-consumption costs. One example is the acquisition of seven S-70 Black Hawk helicopters, together with another 3 helicopters of this type received as part of the Merida Initiative.
Non-intrusive inspection equipment	The Federal Police uses VACIS inspection systems with gamma-ray technology designed to check truck and cargo ship containers in order to identify explosives, weapons and other suspicious items.

5.5 Systematic Operating Procedures: Standardization of Police Duty

The purpose of Systematic Operating Procedures is to regulate police actions and standardize operational criteria so they can be adjusted to the Institution's standards and principles. These procedures have been bolstered by the contributions of well-known international agencies so that, in accordance with the duties of the Federal Police, procedures have been introduced for response tasks relating to the rational use of force, the handling of explosive devices, the performance of special operations and for rescue operations and public assistance. Insofar as the investigative attributions of the Federal Police are concerned, the following deserve attention: Systematic Operating Procedures for analysis, criminal files, fieldwork, operations, communications intervention, covert operations, and for the fighting of such crimes as kidnapping, terrorism, and human trafficking, as well as the tasks of crisis negotiation and management. In the case of crime prevention duties, the most important are those duties that encourage and follow up on public complaints, provide surveillance of high crime areas, guard strategic facilities and fight highway crime.

As a result, the introduction of Systematic Operating Procedures as part of the New Public Security Model favors the professional performance of duties by showing that improvisation, discretionary authority and a lack of procedural systematization impact negatively on the results of investigations.

5.6 Respect for Human Rights: A Principle of Federal Police Duty

The Federal Police supervises its officers to ensure they follow the principles set forth in Article 21 of the Constitution: lawfulness, objectivity, efficiency, professionalism, honesty, and respect for human rights. Both in investigative efforts and operational work, officers should perform their duties while respecting fundamental human rights in the terms of Federal Police Law and with the rational, consistent and timely use of police force, pursuant to the provisions of Article 41 of the General Law of the National Public Security System. To guarantee respect for human rights and other constitutional principles governing the actions of public security institutions, Article 40 of the General Law of the National Public Security System states that officers have the following obligations:

i) To perform their duties with absolute impartiality and without any form of discrimination.
ii) To abstain at all times from inflicting or tolerating acts of torture –even when received as an order from a superior or when special circumstances are argued such as a threat to national security, the urgency of an investigation or any other reason. In the case of being aware of any such acts, officers must report them immediately to the relevant authority.
iii) To abstain at all times from arbitrary acts and from unduly limiting peaceful actions or protests exercised by the public as constitutional rights.
iv) To abstain from arresting or ordering the arrest of any person without the requirements set forth in applicable legal provisions.

Complaints
Attention
Program

To ensure strict compliance with the aforementioned principles of duty, the Federal Police has implemented across-the-board policies ranging from the professional development of command and operational units –based on ethical codes and the promotion of a human rights culture– to programs designed to guarantee respect for these rights in operations, such as controlling prison riots, guarding strategic facilities, controlling public protests and other actions where the relevant authorities require the intervention of police operatives.

A Complaints Attention Program for Alleged Human Rights Violations has been implemented. Its main objective is to receive and investigate complaints and reports of presumed violations that may have been committed by public servants of the Secretary of Public Security and its Decentralized Administrative Agencies so that the corresponding administrative, civil or criminal sanctions may be applied.[52]

---

52. As of the first quarter of 2011, 4,559 citizen complaint files had been opened for human rights violations by public servants of the Secretary of Public Security; 2,943 of these involved officers of the Federal Police. Of the total number of complaints filed, 20 resulted in Special Recommendations and two in General Recommendations (0.5% of the total number of complaints received) by the National Commission on Human Rights and which have been accepted by the Secretary of Public Security. Between December 1, 2006 and March 14, 2011, two Federal Police officers were sentenced for abuse of authority.

A fundamental feature of the effort to achieve full respect for human rights has been the implementation of a new disciplinary regime. This includes sanctions that may lead to the dismissal of officers from the police force when they fail to respect the legal system or human rights (Articles 19 and 20 of the Federal Police Law).

Similarly, as part of Systematic Operating Procedures which regulate and define the actions applied by different areas of the Federal Police when performing their duties, measures are established for preventing human rights violations resulting from police actions. In addition, procedures are included which must be followed when receiving human rights representatives or inspectors and when establishing mechanisms for dialogue with family and legal representatives.

A host of programs and actions have been designed and applied for protecting the rights of crime victims[53] and these include free legal advice and aid, psychological attention, telephone attention for crime victims, and the creation of protocols for respecting human rights and assisting victims. In addition, specialized materials on these issues are distributed.[54]

Disciplinary Regime

Protection of the Rights of Crime Victims and Human Rights Defenders

---

53. The Secretary of Public Security drafted the Model Protocol of Action and Attention for Victims of Crime, which was submitted to the Secretary of the Interior (Segob), the Secretary of Social Development (Sedesol), the Secretary of Health (SSA), the System for the Comprehensive Development of the Family (SNDIF), and the Attorney General's Office (PGR). These agencies signed the Framework Agreement establishing the bases for the drafting of protocols for coordinated action and exchange of information with civil society, thereby providing comprehensive and specialized attention to the victims of crime or injured parties. Similarly, the Secretary of Public Security drafted the Protocol for Telephone Attention for Victims of Violence in Emotional Emergency or Crisis, now being implemented though the System of Telephone Attention for Victims of Crime.

54. The following informative brochures and materials for distribution, among others, have been prepared: "United Nations Declaration of Basic Principles of Justice for Victims of Crime and Abuse of Power"; "United Nations Basic Principles on the Use of Force and Firearms by Law Enforcement Officials"; an informative text on "Understanding the Human Rights of Women"; "Human Rights Norms and Practices for Police"; "Complete Manual of Human Rights for Police"; and "Istanbul Protocol: The Manual on the Effective Investigation and Documentation of Torture and other Cruel, Inhuman or Degrading Treatment or Punishment."

Another important feature is the introduction of cautionary measures requested by the National Human Rights Commission (CNDH) to protect human rights defenders, journalists, and other vulnerable persons.

5.7 Public Crime Prevention

The Citizenry's Role in Fighting Crime

The role played by the citizenry in preventing and reporting crimes in their communities is essential to crime fighting. Shared responsibility with the public is required to recover public spaces plagued by criminality, reduce levels of criminal incidents, and encourage a culture of respect for the law.

Public Crime Prevention and Civil Education Programs

In order to coordinate efforts designed to deal with social problems influencing criminal behavior, the General Law of the National Public Security System includes a mandate whereby the State must develop a "comprehensive policy in the area of public prevention of crime related to the causes behind the committing of crimes and anti-social behavior. Further, it must develop programs and perform actions that serve to foster cultural and civil values in society, and which promote respect for the law and the protection of victims" (Article 2). This prevention plan includes programs developed jointly with other institutions, such as campaigns against drug use, and programs addressing groups susceptible to the committing of crimes or groups susceptible to being the victims of crime.

Citizen Observatories

The Federal Police Citizen Observatories Program was created in 2009 with the participation of representatives from civil society organizations to address specific issues in each state. The goal is for the alliance between citizens and government to contribute to a reversal of the factors promoting violence and criminality.

Youth Sensor Program

The Youth Sensor Program has also been implemented using networks of trained young people. The program was created to prevent and identify risk behavior among peers which could eventually lead to criminal acts. These "sensors" work in their immediate environment, performing public crime prevention tasks and promoting anonymous reports by the public. The program seeks to strengthen community links, encourage respect for the law and crime prevention, and promote relations between government and civil society.

Similarly, the Safe Community Program has been implemented for the purpose of applying long term crime prevention actions focused on high risk and vulnerable groups. Among the major actions included in this program are Community Security Workshops and Programs for Child and Youth Security, Comprehensive Prevention, and Cybercrime Prevention.

Safe Community Program

Finally, workshops and actions have been established to promote gender equality and prevent gender violence. Some of the most important actions in this area include the Program for Institutional Culture using a Gender Perspective, the Protocol for Police Action Relating to Gender Violence, and the creation of the National Database and Information Bank on Cases of Violence against Women (Banco Nacional de Datos e Información sobre Casos de Violencia contra las Mujeres, Banavim – acronym in Spanish).

Gender Related Programs

***

The organizational and functional restructuring described above has increased and strengthened the operational capacities of the Secretary of Public Security. It has also helped increase the logistical, human and operational capacities of the Federal Police. This will allow for a more efficient focus on security demands throughout the country by strengthening territorial deployments and through the use of technological infrastructure and systems that will help coordinate joint strategies with the other forces entrusted with public security.

Conclusions

THE NEW PUBLIC SECURITY MODEL FOR MEXICO

CREATION OF A NEW FEDERAL PRISON SYSTEM

6. Creation of a New Federal Prison System

While the growing complexity of criminal phenomena in Mexico made it necessary to strengthen the technological, human and operational capacities of the Federal Police, the Federal Prison System's shortcomings also had to be addressed. The following pages will describe the state of the System at the beginning of this Administration before going on to explain the strategy used to deal with the problems.

6.1 National Context

To establish the scale of challenges implied by updating the prison system, it is necessary to review data regarding the national prison population and its distribution by jurisdiction, as shown in the following diagram and charts:

Prison Population under Local and Federal Jurisdictions

Figure 6. Prison Population in Mexico
As of the first quarter of 2011

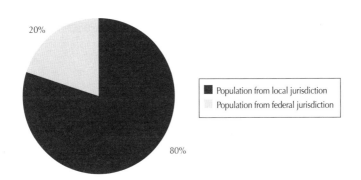

20%

80%

■ Population from local jurisdiction
░ Population from federal jurisdiction

Chart 10. National Prison Population

Item	Population	% Prosecuted	% Sentenced
Population from local jurisdiction	177 577	40.21	59.79
Population from federal jurisdiction	43 854	50.58	49.42
Overall total	221 431	42.26	57.74

Chart 11. States with the largest Prison Populations from Local Jurisdiction
As of the first quarter of 2011

State	Population from Local Jurisdiction	Relative Participation
Federal District	37 170	20.93%
State of Mexico	16 958	9.55%
Baja California	12 492	7.03%
Jalisco	12 304	6.93%
Sonora	9 121	5.14%
Sub-total	88 045	48.58%
Remaining States	86 975	48.98%
Federal Centers	2 557	1.44%
Total	177 577	100.00%

6.2 Condition of the Federal Prison System

Ceferesos

At the beginning of the 1990s the Federal Prison System operated the Islas Marías Penal Colony and Federal District prisons, which during the latter half of the decade were placed under the authority of the Government of the Federal District. By then, the evolution of crime and the emergence of a new criminal profile had already highlighted the need to build prison facilities suitable for high-risk inmates. Consequently, Federal Social Reintegration Centers, also known as Ceferesos, were created. The first center was inaugurated in 1992 in Almoloya de Juárez, State of Mexico, and in 1993 the second was opened in El Salto, Jalisco. These centers are known as Altiplano and Occidente, respectively. This started the move towards increasing the capacity of the Federal Prison System.

In 1996, due to the absence of specialized institutions for inmates with mental problems, the Federal Psychosocial Rehabilitation Center (Centro Federal de Rehabilitación Psicosocial, Ceferepsi) was created and, in 2000, a third maximum-security Cefereso came into operation in Matamoros, Tamaulipas, known as Noreste. In 2002, the state prison center in El Rincón, Nayarit, was donated by the state government and renamed Noroeste.

In 2006 the six centers had an effective capacity of 4,992 spaces. This represented just 3.7% of the total number of beds in the country's entire prison system and 23.4% of the total population under federal jurisdiction subject to processing and sentencing.

Although overcrowding was not a problem, these centers were not immune to the problems typically suffered by other prisons, such as facility deterioration. For the Islas Marías Prison Complex this problem meant the loss of more than 80% of its imprisonment capacity. Islas Marías was originally designed for 8,000 inmates, but had only 1,000 habitable spaces. Despite the fact that the Altiplano, Occidente, and Noreste Ceferesos were created to house the sentenced population, they operated with criteria that distorted their original purpose.

The Federal Prison System also suffered from a lack of staff training and development, and there was an absence of incentives for staff that would encourage a vocation for service and provide them with a future. Most prisons were obsolete, unhealthy, and in a state of deterioration, and also suffered serious problems of overcrowding. Furthermore, no plans or institutions existed to professionalize prison staff or provide training and development.

Ceferepsi

Federal Prison System Problems

6.3 Transformation of the Federal Prison System

It was necessary to introduce policies and actions to strengthen the Federal Prison System. These policies and actions were aimed at correcting shortcomings which over a period of years had served to reduce prison center capacity. The elements guiding and underpinning these actions were:

i)   *Short and Medium-Term Measures*: measures intended to address the prison system crisis by modernizing and updating maximum security Ceferesos, strengthening federal infrastructure, and optimizing the use of national prison facilities. These activities entailed the transference of state correctional facilities to the Federal Government for their operation.

ii) *Building of New Infrastructure:* through the use of public-private investment plans to create a network of federal prisons, the Federal Government was able to assume control of all federal jurisdiction inmates imprisoned at state and municipal prison facilities.

iii) *Criteria Standardization*: criteria needed to be standardized to achieve uniformity in security and operational standards, regulations and procedures. It was also necessary to introduce an objective system for the diagnosis and classification of inmates. Implementation of the National Prison Information System was created for this purpose.

iv) *Prison Career Service:* the purpose is to offer staff a life project with developmental opportunities that favor their service tenure and professional development. Creation of a Career Service is mainly supported by the National Academy of Prison Administration (*Academia Nacional de Administración Penitenciaria*, ANAP), founded in May 2009, and already at the service of the country's prison system.

The Federal Government has performed a series of actions to reinforce the New Prison Model, with the following being some of the most notable.

6.3.1 Federal Prison Infrastructure

i) *Modernizing and updating Ceferesos:* one of the priorities in this area has been to standardize the way maximum security facilities operate by modernizing their infrastructure. During this Administration different types of equipment have been acquired and put into operation, such as: metal and prohibited object detectors, X-rays, drugs and explosives detectors, secure radio communications, cell-phone signal jammers, CCTV and no-break electrical back-ups. Additionally, voice and data networks have been updated, along with federal center servers and access-control systems.

Regarding new spaces for inmates, the maximum use of federal prison facilities has been achieved: Altiplano boosted its capacity by 7.7%, Occidente by 9.8% and Noreste by 3.7%. Together, more than 200 additional spaces were created and a model was designed for custodial staff to provide dignified workplaces for officers overseeing facility security.

Similarly, work has been done on rehabilitating modules at Cefereso No. 4 Noroeste to provide 439 spaces of effective imprisonment capacity. The center currently has 1,360 spaces. Originally designed for a medium-risk population, this prison center has had to adapt to immediate prison needs and currently receives high risk inmates or inmates requiring special protective measures due to threats to their security.

Rehabilitation work at the Islas Marías Prison Complex will help it recover its capacity to house up to 8,000 inmates. Just over 5,500 spaces have now been recovered and repopulation of the complex has already begun –as of the first quarter of 2011 it held 5,266 inmates.

ii) *Incorporation and adaptation of state facilities:* the present nature of federal crimes, which are often linked to organized crime, along with pressure on state prison centers –where security conditions are inadequate– forced the Federal Government to take over control of inmate management at its own facilities. This challenge is one of

Increased Inmate Capacity

Transfer of State Prison Facilities

the most important since it involves roughly 33,700 federal jurisdiction inmates housed in state prisons.

An initial action intended to achieve this goal was the evaluation of projects introduced by states over the course of the last ten years which had not been completed or were inoperative and which could be adapted to a federal prison model. As a result of coordination with states, agreement was reached for transferring six state facilities to the Federal Government. Two of the facilities form part of commitments the Federal Government assumed within the framework of the National Security, Justice and Legality Agreement signed in August 2008.

The first of these, located in Guasave, Sinaloa, is a multi-level facility with a unit for kidnappers and capacity for 900 sentenced inmates. The second facility in Papantla, Veracruz, is intended to be the first prison complex in Mexico with multi-level facilities for inmates representing differing degrees of risk, including a unit for kidnappers. In total it will hold 1,600 sentenced inmates. Transfer of the Monclova Center for Social Reintegration (Cereso) was agreed with the Government of the State of Coahuila and it is currently being adapted to improve security conditions. The fourth facility is in Huimanguillo, Tabasco and has been named Cefereso No. 6 or Sureste; it will have a capacity for 580 inmates during the first phase. Transfer of the Guadalupe Victoria Cereso to the Federal Government was also agreed with the Government of the State of Durango. The facility is known as Cefereso No. 7, or Nor-Noroeste, and began operations in September 2010 with a capacity for 480 inmates.

Finally, the Federal Government, after reaching an agreement with the state government of Veracruz, will take over the administration of a facility converted into Cefereso No. 5 Oriente in Villa Aldama, Veracruz, with a capacity for 2,538 inmates.

The strategy of the Federal Government has led to a 101% increase in Federal Prison System inmate capacity over the past two years. By the end of 2010, the number of facilities it administered had grown from six to eight, with the population of all federal centers growing by 217% over the course of the last year. This means that the task of coordinating states to distribute inmates according to risk level is intense, as is supplying the Ceferesos with inputs for their operation and ensuring the security of facilities.

iii) *Financed Public Works*: considering the lack of public sector resources to provide necessary infrastructure to allow the Federal Government to assume control of all inmates under its jurisdiction in the short term, the exploration of joint financing plans through public-private alliances was necessary to develop the required number of prison centers. As part of this joint plan, the building of eight facilities for the housing of approximately 20,000 inmates has already been agreed. Each facility will have space for 2,552 persons, including two facilities for women. During a second stage, private sector participation will be encouraged to provide prison services, as already occurs in several prison facilities around the country.

To address the federal shortage of prison spaces, work is being performed on three central elements indicated in the following figure:

Figure 7. Central Elements for Strengthening Federal Prison Infrastructure

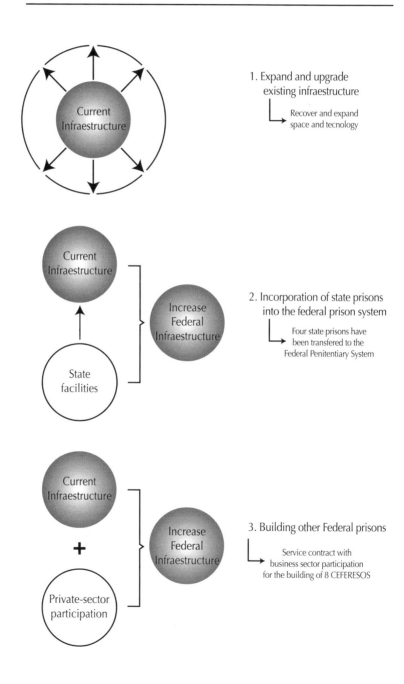

6.3.2 Design of a Prison Career Service

In order for the New Prison Model to operate, a career service was defined with the purpose of professionalizing the performance of prison duties and stimulating staff performance through incentives and development opportunities. Together with the Police Comprehensive Development System, the career service determines the years of experience and knowledge required for advancing through the pay scale, the functional organization of the operation, the mechanisms for continuous training, and benefits for prison staff.

Professional Development in the Performance of Prison Duties

For the training of new officers, the National Academy of Prison Administration commenced activities in May 2009. Its specially designed courses are given to security and custodial staff, and to technical and administrative prison staff. Courses in crisis management will also be given to high ranking and supervisory staff.[58] It was also agreed to give "train-the-trainer" courses at the New Mexico Corrections Training Academy in the United States of America for the purpose of training a staff of professors for the National Academy of Prison Administration. At the same time, manuals and procedures enabling the Prison Model to be introduced were prepared.[59]

An additional agreement was reached with the Colorado Department of Corrections in the United States of America to train personnel in classifying inmates. These trainers, who form the teaching staff of the National Academy of Prison Administration, are responsible for instructing new generations of officers and technicians in the New Prison Model and will train active federal staff to ensure their knowledge is up-to-date.

---

59. From its inauguration on May 11, 2009 to the first quarter of 2011, 1,664 scholarship holders graduated from the National Academy of Prison Administration (ANAP). Of these, 641 officers are prison security officers, 567 are technical officers, and 456 are administrative officers.

60. Close to 370 prison staff have been trained abroad to act as National Academy of Prison Administration instructors and tutors in the practical training of scholarship holders at federal facilities in addition to heading the projects to develop new prison procedures.

6.3.3 National Conference on the Prison System

The National Conference on the Prison System was created by the General Law of the National Public Security System and includes the participation of authorities responsible for social reinstatement throughout the country. The goal is to facilitate coordination and collaboration and to begin joint prison administration programs and actions for the three levels of government. Furthermore, it is responsible for standardizing security operations and establishes the scope of agreements for coordinating and promoting the exchange, registration, systematization and consultation of prison information. Among other actions, the Conference has promoted: a) the performance of an initial diagnosis of technical equipment to prevent telephone extortion from inside prisons; b) a comprehensive report on the prison population linked to the crimes of kidnapping and/or illegal deprivation of liberty, and c) an analysis of the development of the prison industry to identify problems and successful experiences that will help in the design of a plan for its regulation.

6.3.4 New Technological Tools to Strengthen Prison Centers

One of the challenges presented by prisons is the use of new technological tools to help generate intelligence, along with greater effectiveness in operating prison centers through the permanent control of inmates and the monitoring of sentenced persons receiving pre-release benefits.

Electronic bracelets

In order to meet this challenge, the Secretary of Public Security has developed a cutting-edge system to track inmates through the use of electronic bracelets that can be located and traced by satellite through Plataforma Mexico. In addition, this system generates, systematizes and cross-checks information on the behavioral patterns and dynamics of the inmate population to evaluate and improve prison policies and programs.

This technology is placed at the disposal of state governments to help support their prison system programs.

***

Modernizing infrastructure, optimizing the use of existing prison facilities, incorporating and adapting unfinished state works, along with the building of new Ceferesos through public-private investment plans are just some of the actions the Secretary of Public Security has taken to help reverse the decay of the Federal Prison System and counteract its deficiencies.

Along with the aforementioned issues, and considering the evolution of crime and the emergence of new criminal profiles, the standards, regulations, security and operational processes of Ceferesos were made uniform. The National Academy of Prison Administration was also founded to improve the performance of duties by guards and custodial staff, as well as by technical and administrative staff.

Finally, efforts at improving coordination with states were made to counteract differences in the way state prison centers were run, vis-à-vis their federal counterparts. These actions, established by the Secretary of Public Security, have provided a guide for consolidating the New Prison Model.

Conclusions

THE NEW
PUBLIC
SECURITY
MODEL
FOR
MEXICO

COMPLEMENTARY
PUBLIC
SECURITY
RESPONSIBILITIES

7. Complementary Public Security Responsibilities

As a result of the Federal Police restructuring process, it also became necessary to strengthen complementary and auxiliary public security duties fundamental for the proper performance of this role.

Without doubt, a solid police force with duly trained personnel and cutting-edge equipment was needed to provide protection, custody, surveillance and security for facilities and property belonging to the Federal Public Administration (*Administración Pública Federal*, APF), to federal organizations belonging to the Executive, Legislative and Judicial branches, and to constitutionally autonomous organizations, as well as for the protection of the physical integrity of public servants working for these institutions. These needs led to the creation of the Federal Protection Service (*Servicio de Protección Federal*, SPF).

Federal Protection Service

Private security also required strict regulations so that companies in the field would operate efficiently and in observance of the law. This was especially important since private security involves activities that impact the citizenry directly. These activities include the protection, surveillance and custody of persons, information, property, furniture or valuables; the installation and operation of security systems and equipment; and the contribution of data for criminal investigations and support in cases of fires or disasters.

Private Security Regualation

The following pages describe the circumstances behind the creation of the Federal Protection Service and the advantages it offers. There will subsequently be a description of the conditions leading to stricter regulation of private security services and any action taken.

7.1 Federal Protection Service

7.1.1 Protection of Government Facilities: Strategic Action for National Security

The protection of government facilities has become an issue of strategic importance for national security. Guaranteeing their proper functioning has a direct impact on the development of the nation's economic, political and social activities. From this point of view, a comprehensive vision of public security should guarantee the proper performance of government institutions since safeguarding and surveillance cannot be omitted from the government agenda –and in fact require a police force of officers trained to perform this function.

The Federal Government's need for adequate security for facilities and public servants working at these facilities is reflected in the resources earmarked for this category. For example, during the 2006 fiscal year the 193 agencies and bodies comprising Federal Public Administration were jointly allocated 2.941 billion pesos to meet their security and surveillance needs. To put this spending in perspective, Federal Public Administration in this category represented slightly more than 30% of resources assigned to the Secretary of Public Security in 2006, which had a total budget of 9.274 billion pesos. During the same year, the three Branches of Government (Executive, Legislative and Judicial) earmarked slightly more than 5 billion pesos for contracting these services, an amount greater than the total budget of such Government Secretaries as those of the Interior, Foreign Relations, Agrarian Reform, Labor and Social Welfare, and Tourism.

In addition to the resources assigned for these tasks, the need for a professional police force to perform these duties was highlighted by the fact that police providing these services had serious deficiencies, including:

i) A lack of minimum training standards with standardized criteria for their operation.
ii) The lack of a vetting system.
iii) The lack of equipment essential for the performance of their duties.

iv) The predominance of security personnel who did not meet requirements set by the Secretary of National Defense (Sedena) for the granting of a Collective Private License to Carry Firearms.

v) The inability of some police forces and companies to evaluate and determine risk levels that could affect both the facilities they protected as well as their occupants.

These problems confirmed the need for an organization with reliable and efficient personnel. The subsequent creation of the Federal Protection Service was encouraged as a decentralized agency of the Secretary of Public Security, responsible for the safeguarding and surveillance of federal property.

7.1.2 Creation of the Federal Protection Service

The Federal Protection Service was created in December 2008 with the primary function of providing protection, custody, surveillance and security services for the facilities and property of agencies, Federal Public Administration bodies, federal agencies –whether belonging to the Executive, Legislative or Judicial branch– and constitutionally autonomous agencies through the use of "in-house security guards." It is also responsible for protecting the integrity and rights of persons, preventing the committing of crimes and preserving public liberties, order and peace within the sphere of its authority. In order to perform these duties, the Federal Protection Service has mechanisms and systems similar to those used by Federal Police to guarantee the tenure of officers, regulate promotions, provide job security, and follow a strict disciplinary regime.

One of the first steps taken to attract the necessary personnel was the introduction of an Intensive Recruitment Program. Another step was the professional formation of new units through "Basic Training Courses for Internal Security Guards and Bodyguards" which offered training in disciplines such as civil protection, first aid, personal defense, mass mobilization containment, weapons handling, and the evacuation of buildings. Similarly, training was provided to diagnose risk factors and plan security mechanisms.

7.1.3 Technical and Operational Resources Strengthening the New Agency

The methods, procedures, equipping and training standards for Federal Protection Service officers has allowed the Agency to develop complementary strategies with public security police forces. For example, through close coordination with the Federal Police the efficient exchange of information and the generation of intelligence to aid in preventing crime at properties under its protection was made possible.

In order to protect properties and facilities threatened by attempts to disrupt public order, the Federal Protection Service relies on the reactive force of the Federal Police which is a determining factor in dealing with contingencies. One of the resources that best serves this purpose is Plataforma Mexico national network since its infrastructure provides real time information and monitors strategic facilities for the prevention and containment of acts of sabotage and to deal with the effects of natural or premeditated events that place the integrity of facilities and persons at risk. Other essential elements in the design of security strategies by the Federal Protection Service are "strategic facilities maps" and Risk Analyses products which provide technical information that makes it possible to better identify strengths and vulnerabilities inside and outside facilities.

We should also mention that the Federal Protection Service is a self-sustaining agency with an economic consideration scheme that ensures its survival without affecting the institutional budget. During the first quarter of 2011, the Federal Protection Service maintained a presence in 102 buildings belonging to various institutions.

7.2 Private Security

Private security services should strengthen and complement the work of public security institutions. In order for this to be possible, the government must establish and enforce the regulatory framework under which companies providing these services should operate. The purpose is to prevent and, if necessary, sanction any irregularities or illegal practices these companies may be involved in through the implementation of rigorous control and supervisory mechanisms.

From the outset this Administration has implemented rigorous planning, control and supervisory mechanisms, and has applied sanctions more vigorously to guarantee that private security companies subject to federal authorization operate within the law. As a control mechanism for the regulation of these services, the Secretary of Public Security is empowered to adopt security measures (temporary, partial or the total suspension of activities) and, if appropriate, may sanction companies operating at the margins of applicable legal provisions.

The National Register of Private Security Companies, Personnel and Equipment, which maintains a database with current, detailed and reliable information on each company has been updated. With the technical support of Plataforma Mexico, the Register provides additional benefits such as guaranteeing the security and confidentiality of information, the prompt consultation of police records, follow-up and transparency for procedures, and cost reductions in time and resources for both companies and authorities.[61] By the first quarter of 2011, there were 750 private security companies and 68 armoring companies with current federal authorization and revalidation.

Mechanisms have also been designed to standardize personnel training at security companies, allowing them to meet the profile required to perform their duties.

***

The New Public Security Model not only laid the groundwork for the transformation of the Federal Police, some of its features represent a benchmark for institutional design providing support for the operation of the new Federal Protection Service and for promoting the standardization of services provided by federally authorized private security companies.

We have the instruments today to verify that these tasks are entrusted to trained personnel with the necessary equipment to perform their duties, thereby ensuring these services truly complement public security as established by law.

Regulation, Control and Supervision

Conclusions

---

61. In 2006 this registry reported 50,224 officers with full dossiers, while as of the first quarter of 2011 there were 40,000. This is due to the fact that the registry was purged and updated using identification data required to closely follow-up on the records of private-security personnel.

THE NEW PUBLIC SECURITY MODEL FOR MEXICO

FINAL CONSIDERATIONS

8. Final Considerations

With the New Public Security Model the foundations have been laid for the Federal Police and for the rest of Mexico's police forces to adopt an operational paradigm based on the professionalism and reliability of units, the scientific investigation of crime, and police intelligence generation and use for the purpose of coordinating strategies and actions for preventing and combating crime. This Model also offers new tools for effective coordination between public security institutions at the three levels of government through the exchange of information and coordination of joint operations throughout the country. Furthermore, the Model has served as the foundation for an overhaul of the Federal Prison System through the development of infrastructure and the adoption of new mechanisms to guarantee proper inmate control. Using New Public Security Model guidelines as a course of action, the Federal Police can develop its institutional potential and the necessary capacities to consolidate itself as an efficient and reliable police security force. Units that receive continuous training have been incorporated into its ranks and equipment and infrastructure have been modernized for the more efficient performance of its duty to safeguard the security of Mexico and its citizens.

Bases for Transforming the National Public Security System

Fighting crime is a battle the Mexican State should wage jointly and this challenge calls for the shared and decisive action of all authorities involved. The New Public Security Model serves as a benchmark for modernizing and strengthening police forces at the state level, which is crucial for preserving security and public order throughout the country. It should be remembered that state and municipal police represent more than 90% of police officers nationwide and that their responsibilities are essential to efficiently fight crime that does not fall within the exclusive scope of just one of the three levels of government.

Minimum Work Schedule for Consolidating the New Public Security Model

A minimum work schedule for the next few years should include the following topics:

Minimum Work Schedule for the New Public Security Model:

- Adoption of the New Public Security Model for Police Development by all police forces in Mexico. The Police Comprehensive Development System already has replicable processes nationwide to move toward this goal.

- Continuous consolidation and updating of databases comprising Plataforma Mexico network which will strengthen the State´s capacity for police intelligence with the purpose of dismantling the logistical, operational and financial networks of criminal groups.

- Expansion and strengthening of national prison infrastructure.

- Multiplication of actions to boost civil participation in the prevention and reporting of crimes, understanding that the success of State police forces in reducing crime requires broad social support.

- Creation of a technical and autonomous agency with legislative and social representation that follows up the processes for strengthening the country´s public security institutions, thereby guaranteeing their long term viability.

Finally, strengthening public security institutions and reducing crime must be accompanied by the generation of knowledge that contributes to a better understanding of criminal phenomena and the ongoing evaluation of institutional systems and processes introduced to confront these issues. This is why the Center for Security Research and Studies (*Centro de Investigación y Estudios de Seguridad*: CIES) was created. It is a decentralized agency of the Secretary of Public Security which, among other things, is responsible for encouraging academic research to help create new public policy proposals in the area of security, thereby helping to build a national vision of both the patterns of criminal activity and of institutional responses to these phenomena. In the process, this should lead to an increasingly informed debate on public security, and to the strengthening of the institutional tools necessary to overcome this challenge.

THE NEW PUBLIC SECURITY MODEL FOR MEXICO

Se terminó de imprimir en los talleres de Litoprocess
en el mes de noviembre de 2011.
Para su formación se utilizaron los Tipos
Optima diseñada por Aki Kobayashi y
Berckeley diseñada por Frederick W. Goudy.

Para su impresión se utilizó:
Interiores, guardas y portadas, papel FSC$^{®}$ mixto.
Las pastas y lomo cartoné se considera componente
menor por lo que se excluyen de la certificación FSC.

THE NEW PUBLIC SECURITY MODEL FOR MEXICO
was printed by the end of november 2011,
at Litoprocess' Printshops.
Optima typeface designed by Aki Kobayashi, and
Berckeley typeface designed by Frederick W. Goudy
were used for its composition.

The papers used:
For the text, end sheets and cover, mixed paper FSC.
The hard cover is a minor component, is not FSC.